MINORITY
CANADIANS:
Ethnic Groups

MINORITY CANADIANS: Ethnic Groups

Joseph F. Krauter & Morris Davis

n Methuen

Toronto   New York   London   Sydney

Copyright © 1978 by Methuen Publications
A division of the Carswell Company Limited

Canadian Cataloguing in Publication Data
  Krauter, Joseph F., 1919-
    Minority Canadians

ISBN 0-458-92240-4

1. Minorities—Canada. 2. Ethnology—Canada.
3. Canada—Race question. I. Davis, Morris,
1933—   II. Title.

FC104.K73   301.45'1'0971   C78-001046-9
F1035.A1K73

Printed and bound in Canada

1 2 3 4 5   82 81 80 79 78

To Mary Davis, Etta F. Miller and Louisa Krauter

ACKNOWLEDGEMENTS

Our major debt is to various published sources of information. Many of these are singled out in footnotes. To their authors, and to others unmentioned who have provided valuable background data, we express our gratitude.

We also appreciate the typing and general office assistance of Debbie Corzine, Lenore Gray, Cathy J. Reisner, Marsheneal Townsend and Linda S. Wade. Support of a more personal kind was provided by Ruth M. Davis, who somehow managed to get things moving and to keep the sparks from flying.

J.F.K.
M.D.

CONTENTS

Chapter 1

INTRODUCTION

Minority Canadians: Ethnic Groups focuses upon the historical experiences and present conditions in this country of such peoples as Canadian Indians, Inuit, Blacks, Chinese and Japanese, other Asians, Italians, and Ukrainians. Briefer notice is also given Métis, Mexicans, and recent European refugees. All these categories, and especially the non-whites, constitute minorities according to the twin criteria of relatively small numbers and relative deprivation. The two aspects, quantitative and qualitative, are briefly and generally canvassed in this introductory chapter. The rest of the book is a concrete discussion of the way in which particular groups have experienced special and unequal treatment in specific areas such as immigration and citizenship, the franchise, education, employment, health care, and housing. A final chapter attempts a few systematic comparisons among the various minorities.

What Is a Minority?
The two most widely accepted standards for considering a group to be a minority are that its members form a small fraction of the entire population and that they experience marked discrimination. Both attributes involve questions of definition. After all, how small is "small" and how marked is "marked"? Any answer must be arbitrary to some extent. One could, for example, consider Canadian males to be a minority since their sum is less than half the country's population, and Canadian females to be a minority since they are in general less advantaged than the men. From that perspective there would be nobody here but minorities. Such a realization may be morally inspiring and help to instill an appropriate modesty, but since the definition applies to everyone and excludes no one, it furnishes little real information.

So too it is less than optimally useful to concur with Wirth and define a minority as a group that, because of its physical or cultural characteristics, is singled out from others in the society in which it lives for differential and unequal treatment, and therefore regards itself as an object of collective discrimination. Minority status carries with it exclusion from full participation in the life of the society.[1] Even in a democracy like Canada, "full participation" for most citizens remains an ideal rather than a reality. Many may possess some basic understanding of the structure and function of the socio-political system, but rarely have they developed a participant (and not just a subject) orientation.[2] Though

1

happy to receive benefits from the process, they do not intervene in the development and application of policy.

More severe cutting lines should prove more helpful. Henceforth, we will limit the term "minority" largely to groups that each constitute *less than 10 percent* of Canada's total population and that have also suffered, not occasional insult or prejudice to some of their members, but blatant, prolonged, and persistent discrimination. Both characteristics apply conjointly to all the non-white groups, Canadian Indians, Métis, Inuit, Blacks, Chinese, Japanese, Other Asians, and Mexicans or Caribbean migratory workers, discussed in Chapters 2 through 6. Theirs are the truly poignant situations, where great damage is suffered, or in the case of Japanese-Canadians has been suffered, and where the democratic vote process cannot by itself alleviate the harm. On the one hand, these groups are all "visible minorities," their skin colour an inalterable identity badge that singles them out from white Canada and facilitates the planning and administration of discriminatory practices against them. On the other hand, even if aggregated, they fall far short of the 10 percent cutting line we have established.[3] As a result, they are virtually precluded from exercising sufficient influence through the ballot box to ease their circumstances. They simply lack the vote potential of Blacks and Spanish-surnamed Americans in the United States.

In Chapter 7, definitional requirements are relaxed somewhat so that the experiences of Italian and Ukrainian immigrants and of recent European refugees may be briefly discussed. Certainly, they have stood a better chance of blending into Canadian society than have the more visible minorities. Contrasting their fate with that of the other groups illumines the impress of race upon Canadian history. Since Italians and Ukrainians together comprise about 7 percent of Canada's population according to the 1971 census, they are also less disadvantaged by their numerical size.

Any greater definitional precision about the term "minority" would be inappropriate, suggesting as it might that the data we have to work with are more accurate and unambiguous than is the case. On the contrary, the figures available are nearly always open to serious question. As a result, census reports almost invariably undercount the ethnic minorities discussed here. In addition to sampling errors, they tend to miss, for example, illegal immigrants, urbanized Indians, and Blacks who "pass."[4] And recent governmental policy has served in some ways to make the true figures even more indeterminate.

> . . . because of a decision made in 1967 no longer to record the ethnic origin of immigrants—for fear that this might involve some kind of discrimination—and only to record an immigrant's country of citizenship and last permanent residence, we now do not know exactly who is coming to Canada under each national heading, nor can we estimate with any accuracy the current size of ethnic groups in Canada.[5]

While one suspects that recent immigration from Britain includes many thousands whose origins lie in the Indian subcontinent and that entrants from the West Indies are mainly Black, there is no way to be sure.

In addition, inflows into ethnic minority populations occur far faster than the apparent ability of governmental demographers to record, compute, and disseminate information about them. As we write (late 1977), the most recent official material on these groups remains what was collected in 1971—and some of that is only freshly published. The 1976 census is thus far only partially in print; moreover, it did not collect information on ethnicity. As a consequence, a full update would require attaching to the 1971 counts (which, as mentioned above, are often seriously deficient) other correctional factors, often quite rough, in order to make allowance for subsequent birth and death rates, immigration and emigration, and so on. Indeed, the problem is far greater than this if one wishes to speak not merely to the size of these minority groups but to the way their members at present really fare in Canadian society.

There is no satisfactory way out of this social science dilemma. Certainly we possess no solution that has evaded others. For the most part, we merely cite what official figures we can find, trusting that the reader will remember the *caveats* just outlined. The numerical data are mainly from 1971, though some immigration counts, also flawed, are a few years fresher. Occasionally we suggest somewhat larger and more realistic figures, though these are only "guesstimates," even if taken from a printed source, and should be treated as such. Clearly, using finer definitional distinctions on such data would be akin to wielding a scalpel in a butcher shop.

Further ambiguities about ethnic groups reside in the historical record. Information collected on ethnicity has usually reflected certain objective characteristics, e.g., country of origin (apart from Canada and the United States) going back on the father's side, or language spoken at home. The vital attributes of ethnic groups, however, according to many social scientists, flow from subjective identification. As E. C. Hughes has stated:

> An ethnic group is not one because of the degree of measurable or observable difference from other groups; it is an ethnic group, on the contrary, because the people in it and the people out of it know that it is one; because both the *ins* and the *outs* talk, feel and act as if it were a separate group.[6]

Once this latter orientation is adopted, unarguably pertinent data become difficult to obtain and assess. One must, so to speak, know not only how people look but what they feel. The likelihood of fluidity over time also increases so markedly that kaleidoscope rather than mosaic may be a better overall term for Canadian ethnic relations.[7]

In addition, the historical truths about ethnic minorities are no more certain than history as a whole. Long held "facts" may prove to be unfounded or of only narrow application. New facts may be uncovered. Previously unthought-of linkages among facts may be probed. And besides, facts do not speak to us directly. They must be interpreted to have meaning. So each generation must rewrite history, not to falsify or propagandize but in order to pursue questions that seem especially relevant to the times.

The insufficiencies of statistical basis, sociological categorization, and historical record urge a certain modesty of presentation. At the least, all numbers should be treated with caution. One hopes that they point in a generally correct direction. But they are only indicative, not definitive. They are presented as the best that is readily available in order to illustrate events, and not to inspire any sense of false concreteness. Nor do we claim special competence to see beyond the horizon of our own generational confines or into the minds of those who either affiliate or interact with the various ethnic groups. Those who "belong" and those who are younger than we may well see many things differently. If this book helps stimulate debate, that will be all to the good. For it is through such discussion and response that social science knowledge advances.

Natives and Immigrants

All Canadians except native Indians and Inuit are immigrants or the descendants of immigrants. Yet despite the importance of immigration to Canadian development, the country adopted no integrated national legislation on the subject until the Immigration Act of 1952, which took effect on June 1, 1953. Policies toward immigration have existed, however, since 1867, as reflected in a number of individual laws and regulations.

Until the end of World War II, the general trend over time was toward greater and greater restrictiveness. Thus, the Chinese Immigration Act of 1923 excluded all Chinese except clergymen, students, certain merchants, and consular officials. In 1930, Asian immigration was confined to wives and unmarried minor children of Canadian citizens who were already living in Canada and able to receive and care for them. The following year, entry was limited to certain British subjects (i.e., persons from Great Britain, New Zealand, Australia, Newfoundland, the Union of South Africa, and Ireland), United States citizens, wives and children under eighteen of legal Canadian residents, and "agriculturists having sufficient means to farm in Canada."

Since World War II, the tendency has been to widen geographical areas of acceptability while, more recently in particular, invoking new educational and occupational criteria. The Canadian Citizenship Act of 1946 made allowances for war refugees, put French citizens on an immigration par with British subjects, and encouraged the arrival of farm workers and miners. Nineteen forty-seven saw the repeal of the 1927 Chinese Immigration Act; and 1951, the negotiation of bilateral agreements with India, Pakistan, and Ceylon (now Sri Lanka) to admit 150 Indians, 100 Pakistanis, and 50 Ceylonese per year. In 1950 and 1952, restrictions against entry of persons from former enemy countries, Germany, Italy, and Japan, were also lifted.

In 1952, as noted above, the present Immigration Act was passed, consolidating all policies then in effect and giving the Cabinet authority to issue further Orders-in-Council regulating immigration. Thereafter, major changes occurred in 1962, when all racial qualifications were removed, special privileges for British, French, and other Europeans were eliminated, and employability was established as the main attribute for selection; and in 1967, when a "point" system went into effect. Assessment units are now awarded under nine headings:

1. *Education and Training:* up to 20 units, one for each year of formal education or occupational training.
2. *Personal Assessment:* up to 15 units, based on the immigration officer's judgement about the applicant's adaptability, motivation, initiative, etc.
3. *Occupational Demand:* up to 15 units, if demand for the applicant's occupation, skilled or unskilled, is high in Canada.
4. *Occupational Skill:* from 10 units for professionals to 1 unit for unskilled labour.
5. *Age:* 10 units for applicants under 35, with one unit deducted for each year above 35.
6. *Arranged Employment:* 10 units if the applicant has a definite job prearranged.
7. *Knowledge of French or English:* up to 10 units depending on the degree of fluency.
8. *Relative:* up to 15 units if the applicant has a relative in Canada able to help in becoming established.
9. *Employment Opportunities in Area of Destination:* up to 5 units, if the applicant intends to go to an area where a strong demand for labour exists.

The highest possible score is 100, with 60 the ordinary current passing line.[8] The system favours well-educated professional people who already have a relative in Canada to assist them. (By itself, this description should yield about 65 points on items 1 and 4 through 8 alone.) For this reason Canada has sometimes been criticized for draining off educated and skilled people from developing countries, where their expertise is desperately needed.

It is not through immigration, of course, but through a high fertility rate and declining death rate that Canadian Indian and Inuit populations continue to grow. Their age-specific profiles appropriately resemble those of newly developing nations. By contrast, it is recent immigration from the West Indies, Asia, and the nations of the Pacific that accounts for much of the sizeable increase in numbers of Blacks, Chinese, East Indians, Pakistanis, and Japanese.[9] At the same time, immigration from southern and eastern Europe has receded considerably from its high water marks of the 1960s.[10]

In 1969, the federal government initiated a seven-year "Longitudinal Study of the Economic and Social Adaptation of Immigrants."[11] The results of this study undoubtedly help to inform pending legislative action on immigration. Meanwhile, Canada's ethnic balance, and the place within it of the groups discussed here, continues to change.

NOTES

[1] Wirth, Louis, "The Problems of Minority Groups," in Ralph Linton, ed., *The Science of Man in the World Crisis* (New York: Columbia University Press, 1945), p. 347.

[2] For the terminology see Almond, Gabriel A., and Sidney Verba, *The Civic Culture* (Princeton: Princeton University Press, 1963), pp. 16-23.

[3] For a summary as of 1971, see Chapter 8, especially Table II. Indeed, even together the non-white minorities listed there amounted officially to only 3 percent of Canada's population.

[4] Sampling errors are not too serious, since very large samples (one-third in 1971) have been used. Coverage errors are more problematical. For a brief discussion see *Population, 1971 Census of Canada, Introduction to Vol. 1 (Part 3)*, Statistics Canada (Ottawa: Information Canada, 1976), pp. 13 and 21-23.

[5] Hawkins, Freda, "Canada's Green Paper on Immigration Policy," *International Migration Review* (Center for Migration Studies of New York, Inc.) IX (1975), p. 243.

[6] Hughes, Everett C., "The Study of Ethnic Relations," reprinted in *The Sociological Eye* (Chicago: Aldine-Atherton, 1971), p. 153.

[7] See Burnet, Jean, "Ethnic Relations and Ethnic Policies in Canadian Society," a paper prepared for the IXth International Congress of Anthropological and Ethnological Sciences, 1973, p. 8.

[8] Hawkins, *op. cit.*, p. 210.

[9] Between 1968 and 1973, some 33,112 West Indians entered Canada, 46,036 Chinese (including many from Hong Kong), 49,007 East Indians (plus more than 7,000 Asians from Uganda), 7,085 Pakistanis, and 4,962 Japanese. See *Immigration and Population Statistics*, Department of Manpower and Immigration (Ottawa: Information Canada, 1974), pp. 32ff.

[10] Italian immigration declined from 166,379 for 1951-57 to 121,802 for 1963-67 to 54,556 for 1968-73. For the same periods, Polish immigration went from 18,773 to 8,549 to 6,388, and Ukrainian immigration from 3,413 to 857 to 1,323. *Ibid.*

[11] *Three Years in Canada*, Manpower and Immigration (Ottawa: Information Canada, 1974) is the "first report" of this study.

Chapter 2
CANADIAN INDIANS AND MÉTIS

In a fairly obvious sense, Canada is the Canadian Indians' own country. Along with the Inuit, they were well settled here long before the arrival of white immigrants from Europe. Nor can it be said that contact with these newcomers immediately benefited the Indians. Having lived in isolation from the outside world and other societies for thousands of years, Indians had developed no resistance to diseases that had long ravaged Europe. As a result, they frequently fell victim in epidemic proportions to ailments that the explorers and colonists, with their partial immunity, unwittingly introduced. Not only did smallpox take a heavy toll among the Indians after these encounters, but so also did respiratory and social diseases.

Today, the Indian population is again on the rise at a pace nearly twice that of the Canadian population in general. According to the 1971 census, there are 295,215 registered (or "status") Indians. This amounts to about 1.4 percent of the total Canadian population, and marks a notable increase over the 208,286 (or 1.1 percent of the total) reported in the 1961 census.[1] In addition, there are probably over 200,000 non-registered Indians. Not included in these figures are perhaps 250,000 to 300,000 persons of mixed Indian-white descent, known as Métis. Yet even with a combined total of nearly 750,000, Indians and Métis remain a severely disadvantaged minority. Indeed, no other group in Canada has been studied and talked about so much to so little apparent gain.

Even omitting the Métis, Indians have been traditionally classified into six main tribal groups, each with its own culture, and ten linguistic groups, these in turn being subdividable into scores of dialects. This has made it difficult for Indians to organize in a unified fashion. The situation has been improving, however, since the establishment of the National Indian Brotherhood and the Native Council of Canada in the 1960s.

Indians are scattered across the Canadian land mass. Of those registered Ontario contains about 62,415 and British Columbia about 52,220, which means that 180,000 live in the other provinces and territories. They are also distributed among 565 bands, whose populations range from less than one hundred to more than 8,000.[2] Moreover, there are 2,276 reserves across the country, where treaty Indians and their families are entitled to live. Over 90,000 registered Indians, or 30.7 percent of the total, live in urban centres of 1,000 or more, and even such metropolises as Winnipeg, Toronto, and Vancouver contain Indian enclaves. Some Indians who choose to live off the reserve also seek to suppress their Indian identity, feeling that it places them at a disadvantage in white society.[3]

This chapter first briefly discusses the reserve system, which still determines so much of Indian life, the Indians' legal status, which has been shaped over the years by various Indian Acts, and some recent legal and political rumblings in the Canadian North. Attention then focuses on the way in which these people were deprived of the vote for more than half a century, and on present-day interrelated problem areas of education, employment, and housing. Before the concluding comment, a separate section considers the situation of the Métis both in the Northwest Territories and on the prairies.

The Reserve System

On their arrival in Canada, the French made limited and largely unsuccessful attempts to enslave the Indians. The Indian slaves were called *panis*, since the majority were from the Pawnees or from closely related tribes.[4] The inauguration of the reserve system by the French was also an outgrowth of their desire to colonize the native population. Besides affording the Indians some protection against the encroachments of white settlers, the reserves were instruments for Christianizing natives and otherwise assimilating them to French culture.[5] In the process, the French also encouraged Indian antagonisms against the British. For example, one Jesuit missionary instructed the Micmac that the English had crucified Christ.[6]

The British followed the French lead and continued the reserve system. Bilateral treaties were concluded with Indians in order to extinguish aboriginal land titles which otherwise could have been recognized in British and Canadian courts.[7] Indians traded away ancestral lands, lands which were morally and legally theirs, for treaty money, guarantees of educational, medical, and welfare programs, and reserve lands. Many reserves were in areas already occupied by Indians; others were far distant and required tribal relocation. Treaties negotiated later by the Canadian government followed much the same pattern. Reserves were, however, established only in areas where whites wished to enter and expand. There was no need for them in places like Labrador or the Northwest Territories, which were until recently of little interest to whites.

In general, the reserve system met with the approval of the majority of Canadians.

> The treaty system was quite frankly a policy of expediency. It was designed to forestall quarrels between the Indians and whites over land,

to facilitate the spread of white settlements, and to maintain the traditional military alliance with the Indians. It was not intended to help the
Indian adjust himself culturally or economically. This being the object
of the treaty system, it was completely successful. [8]

Yet, as the quotation suggests, serious problems were always present.

Traditional Indian social and political systems were maintained on the
reserves. Originally, hereditary chieftainships were established under
government sponsorship, although today these leaders are elected in
most if not all bands. In either case, their powers in government negotiations have been extremely limited. As a result, although they are supposed to represent the band in dealings with the government, they
serve mainly as figureheads, satisfying the white Canadian expectation
that every group should have its own leader to speak for it.

In addition, few reserves offer much opportunity for employment or
recreation. Even if a reserve contains commercially viable quantities of
natural resources, the Indians lack the capital and technology to exploit
them alone. Location may also make access to medical services, employment centres, and commercial or business establishments difficult if not
impossible. Such isolation and economic depression help explain why
most people on reserves are supported by the government through the
Indian Affairs Branch Welfare Program, old age pensions, unemployment insurance payments, and, more rarely, veterans' pensions and
various salaried vocational or educational programs.

Despite its evident shortcomings, the longer an institution remains in
existence, the more solidly entrenched it becomes. The reserves may
well constitute a wardship system incompatible with a free democratic
society, but many Indians have become so dependent upon them for security that any sudden abandonment could prove highly traumatic.

Legal Status

As defined by law, an Indian is "a person who pursuant to this Act is
registered as an Indian or is entitled to be registered as an Indian." [9] The
Act referred to is the Indian Act of 1970, the latest in a long series of such
documents dating from 1876. The British North America Act had given
the federal government responsibility for management of the Indians.
Canada was then an overwhelmingly agricultural country, with new regions constantly being opened to the plow. Indians had to be moved to
make way for white settlers. Instead of adopting the military massacre
strategies of the United States, Canadian authorities concluded treaties
by which Indians were confined, usually within restricted portions of
their former territories. Agriculture, not fishing and game hunting, was
expected to become the main economic activity for Indians, just as it was
for the rest of Canada. The reserves, it was thought, would be ideal for
such agricultural pursuits.

The Indian Acts are closely tied in with the various treaties made between Canada and the Indians, the most recent of which is probably the James Bay Agreement of 1975.[10] A given Indian's legal status depends, in other words, conjointly upon the treaty, if any, that applies to his tribe and upon the Indian Act currently in force. Over the years, questions relating to both kinds of legal sources have been hotly debated in courts and in legislative bodies. It has been frequently charged that the Indians did not fully understand the implications of the treaties they signed, and that the federal government confronted them with an either-or proposition. This may in fact have been true. Today, however, many Indians look upon the treaties differently: "The view of the contemporary Indian leadership, that treaty rights are of basic importance, may arise in part out of the wish to respect the political power and astuteness of the Indian leaders who negotiated the treaties."[11]

Like its successors, the initial Indian Act of 1876 provided for controls, prohibitions, and restrictions under which hundreds of thousands of people would henceforth live. As a member of the Indian Affairs Branch once remarked, "Probably there is no other legislation which deals with so many and varied subjects in a single act. It may be said indeed to deal with the whole life of a people."[12]

The federal agency responsible for enforcing the Indian Act has varied over the years. The task first fell to the Department of the Secretary of State. Then it moved to the Department of Interior in 1873, the Department of Indian Affairs in 1880, and finally the Indian Affairs Branch. (In general, provinces could regulate Indians only as individuals and not as part of the reserve system.) Under the Acts, the position of Minister of Indian Affairs became an extremely powerful one. His approval was required before an Indian's property rights were transferred or the executors of a will appointed. Of his own volition, he could appeal to the Exchequer Court of Canada to declare any Indian will void in whole or in part.

The Indian Acts have long attempted to legislate morality. Until 1951, it was an offence for any Indian to frequent a poolroom on or off the reserve, where he might "misspend or waste his time."[13] The old custom of potlatching was outlawed until the 1950s. The possession and use of liquor was prohibited to Indians, whether on or off a reserve.

The main result was to increase the Indian jail and penitentiary population. In western provinces it regularly reached 60 or 70 percent of the total. A study made in British Columbia during 1956 explains how this came about.

> . . . offences having to do with liquor, or stemming from intoxication, constitute by far the bulk of Indian offences. . . . Most Indian criminals, in other words, are indicted for offences that do not constitute offences for Whites. If the Indian were as free in his action in this respect as a White person, his criminal record would be much clearer than it is now,

and probably his criminal record would, on the average, be much clearer than for the average group of Whites.[14]

Even recently, Indians in Saskatchewan, who comprise about 4 percent of that province's population, had ten times as many persons convicted of indictable liquor offences as did non-Indians.[15] Their conviction rate, to put it another way, was about 250 times higher than the provincial average.

Numerous protests and court cases have recently brought about changes in the law. Liquor is now generally permitted on reserves, though individual reserves may vote to exclude it. The historic Drybones case of 1967 held that the section of the Indian Act which provided stricter penalties for Indian drunkenness than for non-Indian drunkenness was in conflict with the Bill of Rights. The Canard case of 1975 also concluded that vesting the power to appoint executors of wills in the Minister of Indian Affairs denied Indians full equality before the law.

Other sections of the Indian Act continue to be upheld in spite of their seemingly discriminatory content. Consider the experiences of two women in the early 1970s, Jeanette Lavell and Yvonne Bedard. Lavell, of Indian ancestry and a registered member of the Wikwemikong band in Ontario, married a non-Indian during the spring of 1970. In December 1970, her name was removed from the band list of registered Indians, since, under the provisions of Section 12 (1) (b) of the Indian Act of 1952, she no longer had a right to be so registered. Lavell argued she was being discriminated against because of her sex. In the same year, Yvonne Bedard returned to the Six Nations Reserve near Brantford, Ontario, in order to live with her mother. Born an Indian, she had lived on the reserve until 1965 when she married a non-Indian and left. In 1970, she separated from her husband. At first, the band gave her permission to live on the reserve. But in September 1971, once again on the basis of Section 12 (1) (b), the chief and band council passed a resolution requesting that the district administrator of Indian Affairs serve notice on Bedard to leave. In February of 1973, the Lavell and Bedard cases were considered together by the Supreme Court of Canada. The five-to-four majority decision ruled against the women, stating that the Canadian Bill of Rights did not apply to the section of the Indian Act in question. The angry storms of protest that followed this decision have not evoked further clarification of the Indian Act from either the courts or Parliament.

A White Paper on Indian policy, issued by the federal government in 1969, foresaw the eventual cessation of the Indians' special status. Some Indian claims would continue to be recognized, and to this end the establishment of an advisory Indian Claims Commission was advocated. But the general bent of the presentation went against what most Indian spokesmen had been seeking. For example, the government was clearly not prepared to accept aboriginal rights claims. Claims based on treaties were also looked upon dubiously.

> The terms and effects of the treaties between Indian people and the Government are widely misunderstood. A plain reading of the words used in the treaties reveals the limited and minimal promises which were included in them. . . . The significance of the treaties in meeting the economic, educational, health and welfare needs of the Indian people has always been limited and will continue to decline.[16]

Not surprisingly, Indian reaction to the White Paper was negative. The National Indian Brotherhood immediately issued a statement declaring that:

> . . . the policy proposals put forward by the Minister of Indian Affairs are not acceptable to the Indian people of Canada. . . . We view this as a policy designed to divest us of our aboriginal, residual and statutory rights. If we accept this policy, and in the process lose our rights and our lands, we become willing partners in cultural genocide. This we cannot do.[17]

There have been a few changes since then. Some minor amendments, for example, were introduced into the Revised Indian Act of 1970, giving Indians greater self-determination in reserve policies. Pressure also appears to be building in Ottawa for the gradual elimination of the reserve system. In August 1973, the government also announced that it was willing to negotiate settlements in many areas of the country where this had not yet been done. One stumbling block, however, is that outside the Northwest Territories, provincial cooperation may be necessary on a number of issues. In addition, Indians are now reluctant to advance their claims piecemeal. Instead, as the next section indicates, they are pursuing more generalized and regional strategies.

Legal and Political Trends in the North

Two clusters of events deserve particular attention. One concerns the Province of Quebec's giant James Bay hydroelectric power project that is being built in the hunting and fishing grounds of the Cree Indians. The other involves natural gas pipelines that will be built from Prudhoe Bay, Alaska, across the northern Yukon to the Mackenzie Delta, and along the Mackenzie Valley to the Alberta border, thus passing through lands occupied by Métis, by Inuit, and especially by a number of Indian tribes whose members, including both registered and non-registered Indians, refer to themselves as Déné (meaning "people").

When Quebec's boundaries were extended in 1912 to include the James Bay area, the federal government required that Quebec either recognize the rights of the native inhabitants there or obtain formal surrenders of those rights. Neither procedure was followed. The issue became crucial only in May 1971, when the Quebec government announced its intention to develop the hydroelectric power resources of the area. The Indians of Quebec Association began talks with the Quebec government establishing a framework for negotiating a settlement of their land rights. But within three months, before any negotiations had taken place, the Quebec legislature unilaterally formed the James Bay Development Corporation, giving it the powers of a municipal government.

Privately commissioned environmental impact studies that were subsequently carried out indicated the project would have a severe effect on both the ecology of the region and on the traditional livelihood of the native people. The Quebec government, however, refused to delay or modify its plans, and so, on November 7, 1972 both the Indians and the Inuit of the region went to court seeking an interlocutory injunction that would halt the project until their aboriginal title had been dealt with. After a year of hearings, the Quebec Superior Court, in November 1973, granted their request. A week later the Quebec Court of Appeal suspended the injunction. The Supreme Court of Canada refused to consider the case, and on November 21, 1974, the Quebec Court of Appeal unanimously overturned the judgement of the Quebec Superior Court.

With construction work continuing, the Indians were faced with a *fait accompli*. By 1974, they were willing to settle for whatever they could salvage out of a bad situation. They were granted hunting and fishing rights, some 5,250 square miles of land in some form of ownership, and monetary compensation. Of the total agreement package, Quebec clearly got the better half.[18]

In the Mackenzie Valley situation, where the responsibility is totally federal rather than predominantly provincial, the procedures followed have been quite different. In particular, the Order-in-Council P.C. 1974-641 established a Mackenzie Valley Pipeline Inquiry under the direction of Mr. Justice Thomas R. Berger. Formal hearings, which began on March 11, 1975, were held in some thirty-five communities in the Mackenzie Valley region. They yielded 32,353 pages of testimony and led to what is known as the "Berger Report," issued on April 15, 1977.[19]

The Yukon and the Western Arctic have been the scene of several major transportation projects in the past: the Alaska Highway constructed in 1942, from Dawson Creek, B.C., to Fairbanks, Alaska; the Canol Project, an oil pipeline from Norman Wells to Whitehorse; and the Dempster Highway, linking Dawson City to Inuvik. The Berger Inquiry examined technical, social, economic, legal, and political aspects implicit to the construction of the pipeline. For the Indians of the area, the central issues involved treaty rights and land claims. A "Déné Declaration," adopted by the General Assembly of the Indian Brotherhood and Métis Association of the Northwest Territories in a meeting at Fort Simpson in July 1975, stressed the necessity for a just land settlement, a high degree of political sovereignty and self-determination, and development of the North by the native Déné community rather than by outsiders.[20]

The Déné have rejected the model of the James Bay agreement. They have also rejected the Alaskan settlement model. This latter was designed to eliminate the special status of Eskimos (as they are still called in Alaska) by 1991 and assimilate them into the Alaskan community. Many of the Déné fears are appropriate. Promises of native employment are often empty. Large-scale projects based on non-renewable resources have rarely provided long-term employment for significant numbers of native people. Pipeline contractors and their unions have made it clear that native people are not qualified for skilled jobs, and will be hired only as unskilled or semi-skilled labourers. Moreover, once the line is built, it will need no more than two hundred and fifty or so people to operate it. The Inquiry also brought to light the tremendous social damage that will most likely be done during the construction phase of the pipeline. Information now available from the Alaskan experience with a pipeline indicates that among the Eskimo population there has been a sharp increase in social diseases, in crime and violence, and in the use of alcohol. There was a steep rise in violent deaths among native Alaskans, from less than 20 percent in the 1950s to more than 40 percent in 1974. In one small Alaskan village, the suicide rate went up from two in 1968 to eight in 1975.

Should the pipeline be constructed before Indian land claims are settled? The Déné are unanimously opposed to this. They argue that starting the pipeline prior to a land settlement would prejudice their legal position. As one witness at the Inquiry pointed out, ". . . if the Métis land claims had been settled prior to the construction of the CPR, then the rebellion and all its tragic social and cultural impacts could have been avoided."[21] Mr. Justice Berger concurs in general with this assessment:

> In my opinion a period of ten years will be required in the Mackenzie Valley and Western Arctic to settle native claims, and to establish the new institutions and new programs that a settlement will entail. No pipeline should be built until these things have been achieved.
> It would be dishonest to impose a settlement that we know now— and that the native people will know before the ink is dry on it—will not achieve their goals. They will soon realize—just as the native people on the prairies realized a century ago as the settlers poured in—that the actual course of events on the ground will deny the promises that appear on paper. The advance of the industrial system would determine the course of events, no matter what Parliament, the courts, this Inquiry or anyone else may say.[22]

In early 1977, the federal government named two new boards of inquiry, one headed by Dean Kenneth M. Lysyk and one by Dr. H. M. Hill, to study the socio-economic and environmental impact of a pipeline across the southern Yukon. These two boards focused on the Foothills (Yukon) Project, which had not been reviewed in detail by the Berger Commission. The reports of these two boards were submitted to the Canadian Parliament where the issue was debated in a special session on August 4 and 5. On August 8, 1977, the Cabinet announced that:

> . . . the Government has concluded—as did all parties in the debate last week in Parliament—that under appropriate conditions and safeguards, a Northern Pipeline passing through the Southern Yukon Territory to provide the means to transport Canadian gas from the Mackenzie Delta as and when required to meet domestic Canadian needs as well as to provide immediate transport of American gas from Prudhoe Bay would be in Canada's national interest.
>
> The Government has been advised by President Carter that his Administration is prepared to join in discussions with Canada in order to explore whether a basis can be established for agreement between the two countries. . . .[23]

Both the Hill report and the Lysyk inquiry contained *caveats* and conditions on the approval of a pipeline. The Lysyk inquiry recommended that the federal government immediately advance fifty million dollars toward settlement of the native land claims in the Yukon. It also recommended that the construction of any pipeline in the southern Yukon be deferred at least until August 1, 1981 to avoid prejudicing a just settlement of the Déné land claims.

The Franchise

For about thirteen years in the late nineteenth century, until the privilege was taken away from them, Indians were able to vote. In 1885, in an attempt to hasten the assimilation of Indians into the general community, the Canadian Parliament passed an Electoral Franchise Act, conferring the vote in federal elections on all Indians except those of British Columbia, Manitoba, Keewatin, and the Northwest Territories.[24] The Liberal Party disagreed with that franchise extension from the start, alleging that the Indian vote would be greatly affected by the government-appointed Indian agents on the reserves. The Northwest Rebellion (Riel Rebellion) of 1885 also created apprehensions about granting Indians any voting power.

The Liberal Party Convention of 1893 went on record in opposition to federal voting rights for Indians. During the elections of 1896, the votes of Indians in Ontario provided the electoral edge for one particular Conservative candidate. Retaliation quickly emerged from the then Liberal-dominated Parliament in the form of the Franchise Act of 1898. It provided that qualifications for voting in a federal election would be the same as those required by provincial law for voting in a provincial election.[25] Since no province then permitted Indians to vote in provincial elections, they lost their ability to vote in federal elections as well.

After World War I, veterans' organizations intervened on behalf of the four thousand or more Indians who had just seen military service; in 1924, the federal vote was bestowed on Indian war veterans. Additional

Indians became eligible to vote in federal elections when Newfoundland joined Canada in 1949, since it had never barred Indians from voting in its own elections. The same year, British Columbia extended voting privileges to its Indians. It was not until 1960, however, that all adult reserve Indians were empowered to vote in federal elections.

Education

With the inauguration of the reserve system, education for Indian children was a federal responsibility, but it was left almost entirely to voluntary agencies and in particular to the churches. While a school building might be constructed by the government, the providing of teachers was ordinarily left up to these private groups. Only on a few reserves close to urban areas were no schools constructed and the Indian children instead expected to attend public (or parochial) classes in town. One such situation obtains at the Jasper, Alberta, reserve. For years, educational opportunities there had been a source of concern to both Indian agents and white friends of the Indians. No program had been offered at all until the Indian Affairs Branch built a school on the reserve in 1958 and, even then, school attendance was intermittent and casual. In 1965, the school was closed and the children bussed into the city of Jasper.[26]

The church-run, white-oriented school system established on the reserves had a double-edged effect on the Indians. Although it did provide an opportunity to gain a formal education, the teaching process denigrated Indian culture, alienated the young from traditional modes of life, and provided no practical solutions for day-to-day socio-economic problems facing the Indians. Rivalries between Catholics and Protestants often resulted in competition for converts, thereby increasing social conflicts. Government and the church frequently clashed over policies and practices, although neither possessed a satisfactory understanding of Indian culture and values.[27] The Indians became pawns in inter-bureaucratic struggles among various agencies responsible for administering their welfare. Their simultaneous isolation from Canadian society and dependence on outside authority grew greater.

Indians have not always been eager or even willing to have their children attend school. Formal instruction was at variance with traditional learning-by-doing, elder-to-junior Indian methods. Different forms of coercion were tried in order to force parents to send their children to the church schools. Missionaries advocated that rations be restricted for families whose children were truant. Severe punishments were designated for those who dropped out of school, and police assistance was solicited to retrieve them.[28]

Even today, one of the more frustrating features of Indian education is the abnormally high dropout rate. According to the Saskatchewan Provincial Task Force on Education:

A total of 10,010 Treaty Indian students were in schools in Saskatchewan in February (1969). . . . The most revealing aspect of the
enrollment figures is the sharp and continuous decrease in enrollment
beginning as early as grade 3 and continuing on with increasing speed
until, with Indian students, only .5 percent are in grade 12 and in
northern Saskatchewan only .3 percent. . . . Several conclusions can be
reached about this sad situation. First, the students are inadequately
prepared to continue on in an academic stream. Second, parents are
not encouraging their children to go through school, and the pupils see
little point in continuing school for various reasons.[29]

A similar trend is apparent among those few Indian children who were
enrolled in reserve schools within Saskatchewan. As of September 1971,
there were 458 students in Grade one, 46 in Grade nine, and none in
Grade twelve.[30]

The low educational attainment of Indian children is not due to any
lack of intellectual capacity. Studies clearly indicate that, if exposed to
proper facilities and staffing, they can compete with non-Indian children.[31] The problem is to bring about that exposure. One hopeful sign is
that the number of Indian children attending city and town schools is on
the increase; this is due both to bussing schemes ancillary to consolidated school districts, and to the higher percentage of children from
young Indian families living within cities. Some Indian school committees have also been in operation since 1963, helping involve parents in
the operation of the reserve schools. In addition, the University of Alberta has for over a decade been offering a program in intercultural education that prepares teachers better for situations involving both Indian
and white students and their respective parents.

It has frequently been suggested that grade and high school courses
be developed on the history of Canadian Indians to illumine positive
aspects of Indian heritage. Since most Indian children now attend public
or non-reserve schools, such courses would benefit white students as
well as Indian. They might even dispel some of the myths and impres-
sions created by television and motion pictures.[32] As a report of the New
Brunswick Human Rights Commission has noted:

> By and large, this attitude of the general public has been moulded by
> cowboy-movies which tend to be somewhat short on Indian virtues
> and Indian cultural achievements, thereby also reassuring the whites of
> their physical, moral and cultural superiority. Basically it was a process
> governed by economics. Peace-loving tribes such as the Atticamees
> hardly possessed box-office appeal. Nor were Indians supposed to be
> endowed with the great nobility of character displayed by Chief Broken
> Arm, whose life and death were edifying in the extreme.[33]

Employment

Before the white man came, Indians were self-sufficient. Sedentary or
roving, they were able to care for their own needs. Later, as trappers

and hunters, they traded with whites. When Indians withdrew to the reserves, their employment problems began to multiply. Even in recent years, the situation has improved little.

During 1969, for example, of a total employable reserve population in Saskatchewan of 11,634, only 698 (or 6.2 percent) held full-time jobs. About 1,200 obtained some sort of part-time employment, but the income from such sources would not have been high, given the marginality and uncertainty of livelihoods like hunting, trapping, and fishing. Indeed, fewer than 40 percent of the residents on Saskatchewan reserves were earning more than $1,000. [34]

Unemployment figures have especially ominous implications for Indian youths. On the 840-member Swallow Lake Reserve in Saskatchewan, where half the employable people had earned incomes in 1969 below $1,000, merely 60 percent of the reserve's population was below the age of 20. Most of these youths have yet to exert much pressure on the job market. When they do, their employment prospects will certainly not be bright.

Nor do the probabilities of developing most reserves into flourishing or even self-supporting work centres for Indians seem particularly high. An occasional reserve, to be sure, like Skidegate or Caughnawaga or Oneida, has in fact seen the construction of a large industrial park or community centre. But most are too isolated, difficult of terrain, or lacking in water. With the diminishing wilderness being given over to industrial development, those Indians who earned a living as skilled guides and fishermen are losing their traditional employment. The impact of industry on the environment, with its resultant pollution, has deprived whole bands of their livelihood, as at Grassy Narrows and Whitedog reserves in northwestern Ontario. At the same time, with a few exceptions like the Mohawk, who excel as structural steelworkers in the United States and Canada, [35] few Indians possess the technological skills required for employment in today's labour market.

This helps to explain why the placement program begun by the Department of Indian Affairs in 1957 soon expanded to include the relocation of Indian families for employment purposes. Funds were made available for transportation, clothing, and rent subsidies until the family took hold in its new situation. On-the-job training costs could also be picked up for periods as long as six months, with the Indian Affairs Branch contributing up to 50 percent of trainee wages during the period. Other recent sources of aid have included the Local Initiatives Program (LIP) and funds from the Department of Regional Economic Expansion (DREE).

Circumstances, however, are often extremely difficult for Indians living off reserves too. To illustrate: for that one-third of British Columbia's registered Indian families that resided off reserves in January 1971, more than one in four had not been self-supporting for even one month out of thirty. In 1970, 54 percent of the families had incomes from employment of less than $2,000, and 76 percent less than $6,000. About 30 percent of all British Columbia families had total incomes of $10,000 or more; only 6 percent of these Indian families enjoyed a 5-figure income.[36]

British Columbia Indians living off reserves, in fact, are not just below the poverty line, they are far below it. Even government assistance programs fail to raise many of them above that floor. If one adds to earned income such social welfare payments as old age pensions and family allowances, 28 percent of the Indian families remain below the $2,000 level. A principal reason for these meager results is that social assistance payments are low at best. The *Report* of the Special Senate Committee on Poverty pegged the poverty line at $5,000 for a family of four. In British Columbia, an Indian family of four, totally unemployed, would have received a maximum of $2,862 from all government programs.[37]

Many obstacles impede Indian labour advancement. For example, training of unemployed Indian youth under the federal Technical and Vocational Assistance Act has been hampered by their lack of previous schooling. Attempts to find the trainees jobs on the reserve or in nearby cities also prove difficult. Many reserves offer no possibility of job placement, and in white society graduates often meet with unfavourable hiring practices and severe competition.

By law, private industry is required to have 4 percent, if possible, of its workforce on government contracts comprised of Indians and Métis, but firms are not forced to retain such employees if they become absentees or are otherwise unreliable.[38]

Labour union hostility toward Indians has been reduced as a result of various anti-discrimination programs inaugurated by the Canadian Labour Congress in the 1950s. Long before then, however, British Columbia, the most unionized province in Canada, had formed a tradition of good relations between labour and Indians. Since the 1890s, Indians and whites have cooperated in bargaining efforts there in order to protect themselves against Japanese entry into the fishing industry. By contrast, cooperation between Indians and organized labour has been poor in Quebec. Union influence, for example, lay behind certain adverse decisions of the Quebec Labour Relations Commission. In one well-known case, the United Brotherhood of Carpenters and Joiners convinced the Commission in 1955 that Indian lumberjacks did not have to be accorded the same rights as white lumberjacks.[39] The decision was later quashed by the Quebec Superior Court.

Housing
Housing for Indians has always been among the worst in Canada. As late as 1967, a government spokesman admitted that over six thousand

reserve Indian families were "badly housed."[40] More than half the Indians on reserves live in substandard housing, as compared with a national average of 9 percent. Only two reserve houses in five have electricity, and many lack water or sanitary facilities. Even on the Swallow Lake Reserve, where in 1969 some 94 houses out of 135 did have electric service, there was only one telephone, no sewage disposal system, no indoor plumbing, and no fire protection equipment.[41]

The government has tried to improve reserve housing in various ways. In 1950, for example, it transported disused prefabricated buildings from an airforce base to a Kwakiutl Indian reserve near Gilford, British Columbia.[42] And in 1966 it undertook an ambitious program to construct twelve thousand new units over a five-year period. That program is now complete; such government housing is generally standard and adequate, and has involved low maintenance costs. A few broken windows aside, there has been no property destruction reminiscent of that on United States reservations like Pine Ridge. Still, many reserves are characterized by poor housing, a condition that is likely to worsen as the Indian population increases and the demand for additional dwellings multiplies.

For Indians off reserves, housing conditions are often more unsatisfactory. Indian families working for ranchers often live in shacks on the property. Those who are transient labourers in the larger cities usually find housing in slum areas because either landlords will not rent to them elsewhere or they can afford no better. The situation is particularly acute in western urban centres. Only if an Indian has a trade or skill that affords steady employment and good earning power can he escape this fate and live in a middle or lower-middle income area. A few years ago in Saskatoon, Indians and Métis with regular incomes of $10,000 or so a year were found able to purchase private homes in better white neighbourhoods and to obtain long-term mortgages. Such homes are in good school districts, and the Indians there reap that advantage as well.

The Indian Affairs Branch has also introduced a new housing program for Indians living off reserves. The program basically involves conditional mortgage grants, up to a maximum of $10,000 which are linked to family income and to the ability to meet the repayment schedule. If the Indian (or Inuit) family lives in the house for ten years and keeps up its payments, the balance of the mortgage will be erased. To insure that all standards of the National Housing Act are complied with, the Veterans Land Administration and the Central Mortgage and Housing Corporation must approve the house (or the plans, in the event the building is to be newly constructed by a private builder).

Like certain job placement activities, these off-reserve housing grants have an assimilative intent. Both are modelled on relocation programs of the United States Bureau of Indian Affairs. Certain provinces are also playing a minor role to this end. The Saskatchewan government, for example, in cooperation with city administrations, underwrites the purchase and repair of older homes for sale to Indians and Métis. Veterans' houses, built after World War II, were taken over in one project. As of 1969, eleven dwellings had been purchased by the provincial government for such subsequent resale.[43]

The Métis

During Canada's early years, the Métis were an important cultural and political force on the prairies. The designation Métis, a French cognate of the Spanish *"mestizo,"* meaning "mixed," is applied to persons born from the intermarriages of French Canadian (more rarely English or Scottish) males and native Indian females (primarily Cree). They are, so to speak, "the offspring of the Canadian fur trade."[44]

Originally, Métis were hunters and trappers, selling their catch to the North Western Trading Company. In the 1860s, some Métis moved from Ontario and Manitoba into what is now Saskatchewan, but was then part of the Northwest Territories. The first major military encounter with white men came, however, in the Red River Rebellion of 1869. Under the leadership of Louis Riel, a provisional Métis government was established at Fort Garry, Manitoba. Riel led the rebellion but was forced to flee to the United States when troops arrived from eastern Canada to quell it.

From about 1870 to 1880, the Métis lived in peace and relative happiness under the leadership of Gabriel Dumont. But as white settlers and railroads began moving into Métis territory, conflicts broke out over homesteading laws. The government in Ottawa cut back on rations and farming assistance promised to treaty Indians in the area. Thereupon Métis leaders asked Riel to return from the States, and in 1885, the Riel Rebellion took place. The Indians and Métis were defeated at Batoche in Saskatchewan, and Riel was hanged along with eight Indian chiefs—an act many Canadians continue to regret. Failure of the rebellion marked the end of free Indian and Métis occupancy of the prairies.[45]

Métis originally were, and many still are, people of the frontier. After the Riel Rebellion, many began to move northward into the Northwest Territories proper. Indeed, by World War II, there were two separate major groups of Métis: those still in the prairie provinces and those in the Mackenzie District of the Northwest Territories. Other smaller groups of Métis are scattered across Canada.

Métis on the prairies have kept a more continuous hold on their traditions and history. Of late, some of them—the Red River or southern Métis in Saskatchewan, for example—have been developing organizations to promote their cause. One such group is the Métis Association of Saskatchewan, with its 104 local chapters. Its president, Dr. Howard Adams, is a strong proponent of industrialization. He also advocates greater political participation by Métis: "I think the day is gone when we can no longer say that political issues are something that are embarrassing, and that are uncomfortable, and we cannot be involved."[46]

Much of the power of the Saskatchewan Métis Association is the result of effective organization at the local level. In Adams' words: "We believe that if we are going to move into the mainstream society we are going to move in as a total people, as a total culture and not as exceptions. . . ."[47] Other prominent Métis groups include the Manitoba Métis Federation, the Métis Association of Alberta, and the Ontario Métis and Non-Status Indian Association. There are also several active groups in the northern territories.

In general, Métis in the Northwest Territories have a higher status than those on the prairies. They are respected for their capacity to work in the northern environment. With industrialization increasing in the north, and with the promise of the eventual Mackenzie Valley pipeline proposal, Métis can be expected to assume an even more important role in northern development.

In spite of their somewhat better adaptation to white society, the Métis share many of the Indians' problems, such as drinking violations and high dropout rates from school.[48] In the Northwest Territories, for example, Indians, Inuit, and Métis all show dropout rates by age fourteen of about 28 percent.[49] Moreover, though Métis often intermarry with whites, and are increasingly classified by government administrations as white, in the matter of land claims they tend to work closely with Indians.[50]

As far as the federal government is concerned, Métis are no more than just another of Canada's minority groups. Indeed, in one way they are even less than this, for tabulation procedures for the 1971 census were designed to record "no separate count of Métis as such," but instead classified them variously as "Native Indian (non-band) . . ., English, French, or whatever."[51] There has been virtually no special legislation pertaining to them. The major exception followed the Riel Rebellion. At that time, Métis heads of families were forced to choose between a payment of money and land in return for the extinction of any Indian title they might possess.[52] We might also note that 1,400,000 acres were set aside under the Manitoba Act of 1870, "for the benefit of families of the half-breed residents."[53]

Some provinces with relatively large numbers of Métis have also tried to improve their situation directly. In 1965, for example, Premier Ross Thatcher of Saskatchewan set up a special agency to deal with Indian and Métis problems; it was later raised to departmental status. Only in Alberta, though, are lands specifically designed for Métis use. Eight settlements of "associations," comprising some 1,248,000 acres, were established there in the 1940s under a Métis Betterment Act. Title to the land however, remains with the Alberta provincial government.[54]

A Concluding Comment

Indians have far to go before they will have attained their rightful place in Canadian society. They must continually cope with problems of identity, try to gain a positive self-image, and realize a sense of personal dignity. Moreover, until their dignity is respected by others, there can be no equality either.

As thus stated, the chief problems may seem individual and basically psychological. The most feasible ways of alleviating and rectifying them, however, involve more general sociological and organizational approaches. Certainly, at present Indian unity continues to spread across the country, though much progress is needed before the "Buckskin curtain" can be torn down.[55] Groups like the National Indian Brotherhood and the more militant American Indian Movement (AIM) are among the leaders in this effort. Their attempts to engage the interest of younger people and make them proud of their heritage and supporters of Indian culture also have important implications for the future.

Better education for Indians will help. Political activity by Indians at both the federal and provincial levels may win some benefits too. But ultimately, the success of enhanced education and increased political effort depends upon (and in turn contributes to) economic development.

Many people remain suspicious of such prospects. Certainly, the Berger Report wants to put a control governor on the pace of economic change, at least in the special circumstances of the Canadian North. Thus it opts for balanced development based on renewable resources and diversification, hard though this middle course between stagnation and rampant technological intrusion may be to sustain.

> To develop a diversified economy will take time. It will be tedious, not glamorous work. No quick and easy fortunes will be made. There will be failures. The economy will not necessarily attract the interest of the multinational corporations. It will be regarded by many as a step backward. But the evidence I have heard has led me to the conclusion that such a program is the only one that makes sense.[56]

Some people, including those who view themselves as the Indians' "friends," may think even this degree of economic change goes too far. Industrialization, they believe, will destroy the Indians' cultural heritage. It will produce a "white Indian." Many others think Indian (and Métis) industrialization must go much further. That is the message of an Indian spokesman, Harold Cardinal.

> When we start talking about economic development, there are many people who say if you get into industrialization or into business you are going to lose your Indian identity, you are going to lose your Indianness. And one examines the great experiment of Communist China, and one sees the industrialization of that nation, and one finds that industrialization has not made the Chinese any less Chinese. . . . But unless the Indian in this country is able to assume or achieve a meaningful degree of economic power, economic development, the Indian in this country will always continue to wear the shoes of a beggar.[57]

NOTES

[1] *Canada Year Book 1975*, Statistics Canada (Ottawa: Information Canada, 1975), p. 147.

[2] "A band is a group or body of Indians having in common lands or funds held in trust for them by the government." MacInnes, T. R. L., "History of Indian Administration in Canada," *Canadian Journal of Economics and Political Science*, 12:3, August 1946, p. 389.

[3] Denton, Trevor, "Canadian Indian Migrants and Impression Management of Ethnic Stigma," *Canadian Review of Sociology and Anthropology*, 12:1, February 1975, p. 67.

[4] Winks, Robin W., *The Blacks in Canada, A History* (Montreal: McGill-Queen's University Press, 1971), p. 9.

[5] Patterson, E. Palmer II, *The Canadian Indian: A History Since 1500* (Don Mills: Collier-Macmillan Canada, Ltd., 1972), p. 108.

[6] *Ibid.*, p. 62.

[7] Cumming, Peter A., "Native Rights and Law in an Age of Protest," *Alberta Law Review*, 11:2, 1973, p. 239.

[8] Stanley, George G. F., "The Indian Background of Canadian History," *Canadian Historical Association (Historical Papers)*, Report of the Annual Meeting Held at Quebec, June 4-6, 1952, p. 18.

[9] *Revised Statutes of Canada 1970*, c. 1-6, s. 2(1).

[10] "Probably," because some people make much of differences in implications between a "treaty" and an agreement. See Manuel, George, "An Appeal from the Fourth World," *Canadian Forum*, November 1976, p. 10.

[11] Sanders, Douglas, *Native Rights in Canada* (Toronto: Indian-Eskimo Association of Canada, 1970), p. 109.

[12] Quoted in MacInnes, *op. cit.*, p. 388.

[13] *Statutes of Canada 1930*, c. 25, s. 16.

[14] *Indians and the Law*, The Canadian Corrections Association (Ottawa: The Canadian Welfare Council, 1967), p. 32. Reproduced by permission of the Minister of Supply and Services Canada.

[15] McLeod, J., "It's in the Blood?", *Canadian Welfare*, 50:5, September-October 1974, pp. 16-20.

[16] *Indian Claims in Canada*, Indian Claims Commission (Ottawa: Information Canada, 1975), p. 22. Reproduced by permission of the Minister of Supply and Services Canada.

[17] Cited in *ibid.*, p. 23. Reproduced by permission of the Minister of Supply and Services Canada.

[18] For further specification and comment on this agreement, see Chapter 8.

[19] *Northern Frontier Northern Homeland, The Report of the Mackenzie Valley Pipeline Inquiry: Volume One* (Ottawa: Supply and Services Canada, 1977), p. 203.

[20] "The Mackenzie Pipeline: A Matter of Importance," *Canadian Forum*, November 1976, p. 6.

[21] Russell, Peter H., "The Déné Nation and Confederation," *Canadian Forum*, November 1976, p. 36.

[22] *Northern Frontier Northern Homeland*, p. 196. Reproduced by permission of the Minister of Supply and Services Canada.

[23] "How the Cabinet Reached Certain Conclusions About Pipeline Building in the North," *Canada Today*, 8:7, 1977, p. 2.

[24] Montgomery, Malcolm, "The Six Nations and the Macdonald Franchise", *Ontario History*, 57:1, March 1965, pp. 13-25.

[25] *61 Victoria*, c. 14, s. 5(a).

[26] Bennett, John W., "A Cree Indian Reserve," in Jean L. Elliot, ed., *Minority Canadians 1, Native Peoples* (Scarborough: Prentice-Hall of Canada, Ltd., 1971), p. 106.

[27] Patterson, *op. cit.*, p. 114.

[28] *Ibid.*, p. 134.

[29] Cited in Dosman, Edgar J., *Indians: The Urban Dilemma* (Toronto: McClelland and Stewart, 1972), p. 39. Reprinted by permission of The Canadian Publishers, McClelland and Stewart Limited, Toronto.

[30] Dosman, *op. cit.*, p. 40.

[31] "Education in Northern Canada," *Canadian Education and Research Digest*, 3:2, June 1963, p. 91.

[32] Kinsella, Noel A., *Ego-Identity and Indian Education* (Fredericton: The New Brunswick Human Rights Commission, Department of Labour, 1973), p. 47.

[33] Ferrari, Leo, *Human Rights and the Canadian Indian* (Fredericton: The New Brunswick Human Rights Commission, Department of Labour, 1973), p. 35.

[34] Dosman, *op. cit.*, p. 39.

[35] Chapin, M., "Our Changing Indians," *Queen's Quarterly*, 62:3, Autumn 1955, p. 392.

[36] Stanbury, William T., "Poverty Among British Columbia Indians Living Off Reserves," *Canadian Welfare*, 50:1, January-February 1974, p. 20.

[37] *Ibid.*, p. 28.

[38] Dosman, *op. cit.*, p. 134.

[39] Brierly, J., "John Murdock Limitée v. La Commission des Relations Ouvrières," *McGill Law Journal*, 3:2, Spring 1957, pp. 216-19.

[40] Laing, Arthur, then Minister of Indian Affairs, in the *Toronto Daily Star*, February 3, 1967, p. 28.

[41] Dosman, *op. cit.*, p. 59.

[42] Rohner, Ronald P., and Evelyn C. Rohner, "The Kwakiutl: Indians of British Columbia," in Elliot, *loc. cit.*, p. 117.

[43] Dosman, *op. cit.*, p. 108.

[44] Slobodin, Richard, *"Métis of the Far North"*, in Elliot, *loc. cit.*, p. 151.

[45] Campbell, Maria, *Halfbreed* (Toronto: McClelland and Stewart, 1973), p. 11.

[46] Cited in Davis, Arthur K., *Canadian Confrontation* (Banff: Proceedings of the Eleventh Annual Meeting of the Western Association of Sociology and Anthropology, Banff, Alberta, December 28-30, 1969), p. 16.

[47] *Ibid.*, p. 13.

[48] Cardinal, Harold, "The Unjust Society: The Tragedy of Canada's Indians," in Elliot, *loc. cit.*, p. 134.

[49] Clifton, Rodney A., "The Social Adjustment of Native Students in a Northern Canadian Hostel," *Canadian Review of Sociology and Anthropology*, 9:2, May 1972, p. 164.

[50] Slobodin, *op. cit.*, p. 158.

[51] *1971 Census of Canada, Population, Introduction to Volume 1 (Part 3)*, Statistics Canada (Ottawa: Information Canada, 1976), p. 19.

[52] Dosman, *op. cit.*, p. 12.

[53] *Statutes of Canada 1870, 33 Victoria* c. 3, s. 31.

[54] Sanders, *op. cit.*, p. 147.

[55] The term is Cardinal's (*op. cit.*, p. 140).

[56] *Northern Frontier Northern Homeland*, p. xxvi. Reproduced by permission of the Minister of Supply and Services Canada.

[57] Davis, *op. cit.*, p. 22.

Chapter 3
INUIT

The word "Eskimo" (or "Esquimaux") is of Indian origin and means "raw meat eater." French missionaries adopted the term and applied it to natives of the northernmost areas. These people, however, who shared territory, customs, and albeit with some dialect differences, language, called themselves "Inuit," which simply signifies "People." Nowadays, "Inuit" (the singular is "Inuk") is supplanting "Eskimo" even on the tongues of outsiders, and it is the designation that we shall apply throughout this chapter.

The old boundary between Inuit and Indian once lay somewhat below the tree line, which was then considerably south of its present location. Introduction of firearms by whites caused a drastic relocation. Armed with these new weapons, Indians were able to drive the Inuit from the Gulf of St. Lawrence region, and from other areas where life was relatively hospitable, into frozen wastelands that even the Indians were reluctant to enter. Something of an about-face is now taking place, however, with Inuit moving into population centres built for them by the government or even migrating south of the Arctic Circle.

According to the 1971 census, some 17,550 Inuit live in Canada, an increase of nearly 50 percent from the 1961 figure of 11,835.[1] Their present numbers stand at 18,300. About half are found in the Northwest Territories, another 3,800 in Quebec, and most of the remainder in Labrador and in northern portions of the prairie provinces. Closely related people live in the adjacent Arctic lands of eastern Siberia, Alaska, and Greenland.

This chapter discusses first the traditional social structure that the Inuit brought with them into the twentieth century and the legal status that Canadian legislation has conferred upon them. Then various problem areas such as education, jobs, housing and community relocation, and health are outlined. The chapter concludes with a cross-national assessment of Canada's treatment of the Inuit.

Traditionalism and Beyond

Inuit have long grouped themselves in band-type organizations. Each band typically numbered from two to twelve families that hunted and trapped in the same area. Bands were formed around a dominant individual, and occasionally around a shaman who was able through ruthlessness or fear of sorcery to wield power. Order usually prevailed within bands. When belligerent behaviour did occur, it was considered the action of persons not responsible for what they did. This attitude still prevails: it is commonly held that one who is drunk bears no responsibility for his actions, and therefore an Inuk who wishes to injure another frequently gets drunk first. In some instances the community judges the wrongdoer not so much on his objective act as on his total social position in the band. If the community wishes to rid itself of an undesirable member, it may employ either social ostracism or continuous ridicule to force him to conform or to leave.[2]

Authority in Inuit settlements is exercised even today in traditional ways. Parents tell children what to do, older children tell younger ones, and so on. In camps with no single dominant family, overall leadership is taken by some person who by common consent knows the local terrain best, or has been the most successful hunter. Authority among the Inuit, though, is mainly domestic and informal, and is rarely backed by the use of force. Inuit are, in fact, characteristically adverse to giving and accepting commands. Community decisions emerge more from discussion and exchange of views than from edicts of band leaders who exercise only slightly more influence than the other members. Not only are individual Inuit notably independent-minded, but authority does not extend beyond the immediate group. The idea that one person may speak for or command large numbers of people to whom he is not related by kinship or band is completely foreign to their culture. There are no precedents in Inuit history for centralized leadership.

Traditional Inuit society did not need any elaborate governing structure. There were no large residential centres. Division of labour was based simply on sex and age. Members of a band came from the same family, and there was equal access to band resources. Today, by contrast, the Inuit are living under conditions for which the traditional approaches are inadequate. Forced to change from nomadic ways to permanent and semi-permanent communities where the populations run well over a hundred and family ties do not link everyone, they have become more dependent upon outside leadership and direction.

Migration and relocation have characterized the Inuit style for thousands of years. Such nomadic ways prove now to be both an asset and a liability. The tradition of spatial mobility enables the Inuit to make an easier transition into the technological world of the twentieth century. The necessary moves and changes are viewed as just another episode in their trek through history. Inuit adaptability has permitted them to shift easily from temporary hunting and fishing camps to permanent homes in towns and villages. The biggest liabilities are the informal family structures and the lack of strong extra-familial leadership that makes the Inuit unheard in a society where only political and economic influence is listened to.

Until World War II, Inuit contact with the outside world was mediated chiefly by the RCMP, Christian missionaries, and traders from the Hudson's Bay Company. When the war brought about the construction of large airbases at Goose Bay, Churchill, and Frobisher Bay, Inuit and white Canadians came into direct contact for the first time. Inuit labourers and their families became painfully aware of occupying a have-not position in Canadian society. They could easily contrast their own harsh and impoverished way of life with that of the other groups. Of even greater importance to awakening Canadian interest in the Inuit were the white construction workers and military personnel, who on returning south from their assignments publicized the plight of these native people with first-hand details. Articles began to appear in newspapers and magazines within Canada and abroad, exposing the government's inadequate care and treatment of the Inuit people. Since then, the further development of military installations in the North, and the discovery and exploitation of mineral wealth there, have helped keep the Inuit from sliding back into obscurity.

Legal Status

Under section 4(1) of the Indian Act, Inuit are not considered to be Indians or to be subject to the provisions of the Indian Act: "A reference in this Act to an Indian does not include any person of the race of aborigines commonly referred to as Eskimos." This, however, does not put the Inuit beyond the reach of other federal legislation intended for all native people. Section 91(24) of the British North America Act gave the federal government legislative jurisdiction over "Indians and lands reserved for Indians." A Supreme Court of Canada decision in 1939 held that Inuit were "Indians" within the meaning of section 91(24).[3] No reserve lands were set aside for the Inuit, however, nor (with one minor exception) were any treaties signed with them. In 1956 an amendment to the Citizenship Act gave them the franchise.

Although formally a federal responsibility, the Inuit generally had to make do on their own. They were expected to continue living off the land as they had done for centuries, with only the Hudson's Bay Company, other trading firms, and missionaries supplying additional care. The extent to which the government sloughed off its obligations is indicated in its policy about permits to establish trading posts.

> In dealing with applications for permits to establish posts in outlying districts, the Department has stipulated that the applicants must assume full responsibility for the welfare of the natives who trade with them and that destitute natives must be maintained without expense to the Department.[4]

Despite the jurisdiction that it admits to, the federal Parliament has passed no special legislation for Inuit comparable to the Indian Act. Nor, as noted above, has it been much more assiduous about administrative assistance. According to Jenness, the Canadian government "had abdicated most of its duties as the moral (if not the legal) guardian of the Eskimos, and was concealing its neglect beneath a cloak of deceptive or pious phrases."[5] Certainly the RCMP's registering of Inuit births was by itself hardly sufficient.

In 1946, however, the federal government began formulating a more effective set of social policies for Inuit and Indians. Under the direction of Dr. H. L. Keenleyside, who had been named Commissioner of the Northwest Territories, an agency was created to provide them with federal care. Keenleyside also proposed that responsibility for native peoples be assigned increasingly to the various provinces as those peoples became progressively more integrated into mainstream Canadian society. Meanwhile, Inuit matters were elevated in the federal administrative structure when a Department of Northern Affairs and Natural Resources was formed, with an Arctic Division that focused on the Inuit.

Education

Before white men arrived, education for Inuit children meant learning-by-doing. There was no need for, or knowledge of, reading and writing, since verbal communication sufficed in small-group settings. Vocational skills were limited to what the bands required. With the coming of French settlers and their missionaries, schools were organized, chiefly to impart religious instruction (i.e., hasten the conversion to Catholicism of) to Inuit youth. Secular skills and vocational training remained low-priority items.

After the British took control, religious schools continued to form, though they were now outgrowths of the Anglican church. Until the end of World War II, the Inuit remained chiefly dependent for their education on these Catholic and Anglican mission schools. Given the limited resources available to churches in the area, however, such classes were able to serve only a small fraction of the Inuit children.

It would be untrue to say that the federal government had no hand in educating Inuit during the latter half of the nineteenth century. As early as 1873, it paid salaries of teachers in mission schools at Norway House and Nelson River. Moreover, as a consequence of federal responsibility for Indian affairs, by 1887 some 44 reserve day schools and five boarding schools also serviced certain Inuit.

Federal subsidies to church schools for the Inuit began after World War I, though the amounts involved were so small that they could have no marked effect in upgrading existing educational levels. During 1922-23, the federal government contributed a total of $3,000 to all church schools in the Northwest Territories. By 1930-31, the subsidy had increased only to $12,787. A survey taken in 1944 revealed that 93 percent of Inuit and Indian children living in the Mackenzie Delta and the western Arctic were receiving no formal education at all.[6] It is little wonder then that a study from the late 1950s revealed that fewer than five out of every hundred Inuit adults were able to read or write.[7] Only in 1947, in fact, did the federal government begin constructing a public school system for the northern region. Elementary schools were provided for the larger communities, with an especially well-equipped structure in the new model town of Inuvik.

For years there have been two opposing views on the education of native children. One view, while assenting to a formal curriculum, emphasizes the maintenance of traditional cultural patterns and preparation for available employment opportunities. The idea is that what is learned should fit the local milieu. According to the other view, Inuit children should receive an education qualitatively similar to that of other Canadians. Not only does a technologically advanced nation need uniformity in basic education, but also those who lack modern skills are doomed to be left far behind. This conflict of intentions still exists in Inuit education.

When Inuit children first enter formal school, they often experience cultural shock. Besides being enclosed in an unfamiliar environment, they are hemmed in by a degree of discipline and regimentation not required at home. Methods of learning are different, also. Instead of learning by observation and experience, they must now master rationalized rules and procedures.

Like consolidated school districts in southern Canada, which usually require bussing, educational institutions in the north have had to relocate students in order to concentrate them at school locations. Sometimes the methods are quite drastic. Many Inuit children are brought to communities like Inuvik and Yellowknife in early fall and do not return home until spring. Small aircraft search Arctic coasts and islands for nomadic encampments and gather the youngsters found there into marshalling centres, from which larger aircraft can fly them the rest of the way. A journey of up to fifteen hundred miles may result. Residency during the academic year is generally in Anglican or Catholic hostels, with the federal government paying the costs of room and board.

The residential arrangements at other schools may vary somewhat. For example, when a federal day school was opened in the Balser Lake region of the Northwest Territories, seventeen of the students were boarded with Inuit settlement families.[8] Another plan involved placing a half-dozen children in each of several federally built houses, the houses in turn being managed by Inuit couples.[9] Boarding-out systems like these avoid many of the shortcomings associated with institutional housing. The lengthy periods away from parents and the community, however, still cause difficulties. The student in effect is torn between two worlds: the school with its strange environment and his parental home with its traditional culture and often impoverished living standards.

One of the more remarkable aspects of Inuit speech is its relative uniformity over large areas. The language spoken, Inuktituk, has two major subdivisions: Inupik, which is used all the way from Greenland across northern Canada and Alaska to the mouth of the Yukon River; and Yupik, which is employed south and west of this area, including parts of the Yukon and British Columbia, as far as the east coast of Siberia.[10] A single alphabet was fully developed in 1972, and standardized writing introduced in 1976. Mastery of the English language poses remarkably few problems for younger Inuit children.

If they enter school at the age of six or seven, they generally require only about a year of intensive language training in order to become bilingual. They can then carry the same program as children who speak English at home. The later children begin school, the more troublesome the language transition becomes.

The general unavailability of Inuit teachers frequently proves more awkward. Some of the white instructors who fill the gap are non-Canadians, unfamiliar with both Canadian teaching methods and traditional Inuit culture, while those from southern Canada often lack prior teaching experience. Except for a short orientation course in Ottawa, neither group receives any special training or guidance in how to relate to the Inuit environment. Once in the North, moreover, these teachers generally live apart from the Inuit and their rapport with students and parents is often poor.

> There is much evidence to suggest that teachers in schools for Indian and Eskimo children in North America tend to be parochial, compulsively conventional, prejudiced against pupils in their classrooms, shockingly unaware of the differences between cultures of themselves and their children, and lacking in respect and appreciation for the culture of the children they teach.[11]

In the past, little in the way of adult education was provided for the Inuit. They were taught virtually nothing about the workings of the fur trade or the general structure of Canadian government. The sole volume designed for their use was the *Eskimo Book of Knowledge*, printed in English and Inuit by the Hudson's Bay Company in 1931 for distribution throughout the eastern Arctic. Though chiefly intended to improve the Company's fur receipts, the book did provide information about health, savings, game conservation, and changes coming to the North. "What the book says, and the fact that a business company found it necessary to print it, shows how little in 1931 the Canadian government was doing toward native adult education."[12]

Gradually, concern with educating Inuit adults has increased. Even before World War II, Moravians in Labrador included both adults and children in their community education programs. After the war, Manitoba and Saskatchewan also began reaching out in that direction. In 1950, the federal government published a booklet to help Inuit with elementary English and budgeting. In 1959, certain northern cooperatives began diffusing new information among the Inuit. In 1964, the so-called "Q-book" which explained many things about government, health, and education was issued in English and Inuit.

Increasingly, books are being written by and for native people about their history, life, and land. Inuit as well as Indians benefit from this trend and from several other related ones. For instance, the University of Saskatchewan and Trent University in Peterborough, Ontario have inaugurated native studies programs. The Native North American Studies Institute in 1973 opened a college which is attended mainly by native students and directed by native personnel. The Inuit Cultural Institute was founded in 1976 at Eskimo Point. Integrated schools such as Sir John Franklin High School in Yellowknife are helping also to lower racial barriers among Inuit, Métis, and Indians, as well as between these groups and whites.

Also of interest is the experiment begun during 1970 in eleven communities of Arctic Quebec. There Inuit are being employed as teachers for the first three years of the school program. (Through the third year, the language of instruction is Inuktituk; thereafter, it has been either English or French.) The Inuit teachers originally hired under the plan lacked college training, but they were given a three-month training course before being assigned to their classes in kindergarten or grades one and two. In addition, summer courses have been made available to these teachers in order to prepare them for an eventual university degree. The hope and expectation is that by 1980 they will be qualified to teach anywhere within Quebec's provincial school system.

Employment

Traditionally the Inuit were self-sufficient, supporting themselves and their families through hunting and fishing. With the arrival of whites and the Hudson's Bay Company, the Inuit concentrated on the fur trade. Prosperity levels fluctuated considerably because of variations in both the harvest of skins and world market prices. Apart from a few jobs at police or trading stations, there was no other remunerative employment for the Inuit prior to World War II.

A new lease on economic life was initiated by the war. Highways, airfields, and weather stations were constructed in Inuit territory. For the first time, sizeable numbers of Inuit workmen were paid in cash instead of in goods or credit. In line with Northwest Territorial Council recommendations, these workers were hired at only two dollars a day plus housing and rations. The Council also urged that the Inuit be retained in such military jobs for no more than three years, "lest they lose some of their hunting skills and become incapable of living off the country."[13] Even at the two-dollar-a-day rate, those working in construction were earning far more than those hunting or fishing, a fact that created some tensions among the native people.

Surplus clothing, food, furniture, and machines from the military later became available to the Inuit. The amounts were sometimes substantial. For example, from 1949, when the Americans left, until 1962, the Inuit of Ungava operated their boat motors on fuel left behind at Fort Chimo.[14] Clearly, the war had jolted parts of the northland out of those simpler days of rule by the "Big Three": police, trader, and missionary.

In 1955, work began on the DEW Line (Distant Early Warning Line) which girdled the Arctic coast with a network of radar stations and airstrips. To the south, the Mid-Canada Line, another defence network, passed directly through Inuit territory. Inuit workers were used on both construction sites. This time, they were paid standard wages and given relatively equal opportunities in respect to employment. As a result of this construction activity, the rest of the country came to learn more about the Inuit situation.

Employment opportunities have also occurred in the private sector. Nickel and asbestos mines have opened—though some closed not long afterwards. Other Inuit workers are finding jobs in Arctic gas and oil exploration, the federal government having stipulated that at least half the labourers on future pipeline construction and maintenance work in the area must be from the native population. Should light industries be established in the North, Inuit would benefit from the Fair Practices Ordinance of 1966, which prohibits discrimination within the Northwest Territories in accommodations, employment, and trade union membership on the basis of race, creed, colour, nationality, ancestry, or place of origin.[15]

Even so, government service still seems at present to offer the best prospects for Inuit employment. The trend in this direction was signalled in 1951, when the Northwest Territories Council, which dates from 1877, was altered to include elected members and the decision was made to meet in the North as well as in Ottawa. Council headquarters are now at Yellowknife, and five of the newly elected members are natives of the Territory.

As noted earlier, Inuit have historically been an adaptive people. Their development of cooperatives confirms this judgement. These structures—in fur marketing, fishing, retailing, as well as in the production and sale of native arts and crafts—are required to become independent of government and to administer their own affairs as quickly as possible. By 1963, more than six hundred Inuit, or in other words nearly one family in five, held membership in cooperatives, whose total turnover was approximately one million dollars.

The largest and best known of the cooperatives is the West Baffin Eskimo Cooperative at Cape Dorset. Begun in 1959 with assistance from the Northern Affairs Department, it helps meet the demand for Inuit crafts in the United States and Canada. A growing number of Inuit with artistic ability are producing carvings of ivory and soapstone for sale through such cooperatives. A reasonably adept carver can earn up to $100 for twenty hours of work. Alternatively, if the government supplies materials the Inuit must sell the resulting products through the Arts and Crafts Centre, a government agency. The artist receives most of the proceeds from sales, except for a small percentage which goes for Centre maintenance.

Inuit cooperatives, whose principles of sharing in decisions and benefits closely fit the traditional Inuit way of doing things, now number about 40.[16] Their most respected members are the hunters and trappers who, with little or no formal education, have taken on tasks like accounting, management, pricing, and marketing. The talent and drive of these members quickly allowed the cooperative effort to grow large enough to warrant the forming of regional federations. Besides enabling native people to have integrated control over a complex of cooperatives, these federations can also augment their resource base. For example, the Northern Quebec Federation started its own marketing service in southern Canada, while the Northwest Territories Federation has taken over a non-profit marketing company based in Ottawa.

As with most new ventures, some failures do occur. Over-production or debasement of carving can result in a glut of unsold articles. Another danger lies in the possibility of mass-produced, factory-made imitations to compete with the work of the Inuit. A more subtle shortcoming involves unmet needs. To illustrate, few cooperatives concern themselves with housing construction. Yet, if strong financial support should become available from the government, this sort of endeavour would not only generate employment and income, but would also help alleviate the serious housing problems facing the Inuit.

Most of the cooperatives are single-purpose. A few, like the Povungnituk Cooperative in Arctic Quebec, which has a carving branch, a print shop, a fishing branch, a sewing branch for garments, a tourist branch, a modern store, and a credit union, are more complex. Even here, staff is about 98 percent Inuit. While all these cooperatives were founded or instigated by non-natives from the outside, decisions are made collectively by the members, and local people provide virtually the entire working force. As Frank Vallee has remarked: "I cannot stress strongly enough the adult educational value of far northern co-operatives; even if they made no money at all, I would strongly support the movement because of its educational and emancipating consequences."[17] These cooperatives have done much to increase Inuit pride, and to foster interest in their culture among white Canadians.

Housing and Community Relations

When the Inuit led a nomadic life, permanent housing would have been a contradiction in terms. Now that they have generally become more settled, their need for housing has increased. Two difficulties have resulted: one concerns the quality of individual houses, while the other concerns the location of entire communities. Although these two aspects are interconnected, we will in this brief discussion consider them separately.

Substandard housing is almost a trademark of Inuit settlements and the overall tendency since World War II has been for the situation to become worse. In a hostile climate, such housing has contributed substantially to disease, infant mortality, and early death. Differentiations in shelter, moreover, are fostering new class distinctions among the Inuit, as their accommodations run the gamut from tents, shacks, and igloos to prefabs and to multi-room cooperative houses like the Sisi Housing Co-op in Frobisher Bay.

During 1955, the federal government began building a fifty million dollar model community at Inuvik in the Northwest Territories. While engineering and construction difficulties were encountered in the project, good housing is now available there for both Inuit and Indians. Ten years later, the Department of Northern Affairs announced a program under which a further sixteen hundred prefabricated houses would be constructed in various areas of the North. Under present policy, rent paid for housing by Inuit families varies according to means. Those on welfare pay only two dollars a month, and in any case rent cannot exceed 20 percent of the family income. Rent money is credited toward the purchase price of the house, should the occupants decide to buy it.

Clearly, the establishment of Inuit in permanent settlements was necessary and inevitable. That lesson was learned in the immediate aftermath of World War II. The cessation of highway and military projects threw many Inuit back to reliance on the land. But often the land could no longer support them, or else they had lost the will and talent to carry on the old ways of tapping nature directly. Some help was received from governments, churches, and civic organizations, but needs were far outstripping such assistance.

One answer lay in relocating people near better hunting grounds or places of employment. In 1955, for example, Inuit families from Port Harrison, Quebec and from Pond Inlet on Baffin Island were moved northward to new settlements at Resolute Bay and Grise Fiord. Wildlife was more plentiful there and a few jobs were available at the Resolute air base. The people had to learn to adapt to the longer winters and ice cover. It took two years for the two original groups, each with a somewhat different dialect, to mingle.

Other instances of community transfer occurred in Newfoundland, where the government has closed many poor fishing villages and sent the inhabitants to larger settlements. Sometimes groups also move on their own. In 1959, there was a serious and increasing shortage of seals, fish, and firewood in the vicinity of Hebron, Labrador. With the government aware of the situation but not ready to act, some twenty families jumped the gun and burnt down their old houses. They then had to wait in tents until an airlift could be arranged to fly them and thirty other families from the area to towns further south, where some fast house-building had taken place.[18]

Sometimes relocation may take place under near-panic conditions. In 1958, famine and then starvation struck an entire settlement at Garry Lake, Northwest Territories. Royal Canadian Air Force planes evacuated the survivors to a rehabilitation centre at Rankin Inlet, on the west coast of Hudson Bay. Because of the probability of famine spreading, two other groups from nearby camps were airlifted at almost the same time to the Baker Lake settlement.

An analogous problem arose out of the construction of the Great Slave Lake Railway between 1961 and 1965. Some 137 Inuit workers who were employed on the project lived in bunk-cars and trailers.[19] This "temporary" housing was, however, generally better than what was available in the workers' home areas. As a consequence, the Inuit were reluctant to return to their original settlements. Yet they were also unable to maintain themselves in their new surroundings once the project was completed and no further work was available.

Health

In 1900, when about half the northern Indians were within canoe range of some mission hospital or government clinic, there were still no doctors or hospitals in Inuit territory. Not until 1926 and 1927 did the Anglican and Catholic churches each build hospitals at Aklavik in the Northwest Territories. Before 1946, the number of hospitals had increased to four, all church-operated and understaffed. Indeed, as late as 1939, the federal government was spending just $29,480 per year on Inuit care, or about four dollars per head.

The lack of medical facilities and care—in combination with a rigorous climate, inadequate housing, chronic malnutrition, and low resistance to the white man's diseases—took a heavy toll in human life. In 1944, some 48 of 170 victims of an Inuit diphtheria epidemic died. A 1945 survey revealed that 84 percent of 729 recent deaths among Arctic Inuit occurred with neither a doctor nor a nurse in attendance.[20] In 1956, the Inuit population included 1,600 known cases of tuberculosis. Even more recently, the birth and death rates of Inuit have continued to resemble those of many developing countries, with a birth rate two and a half times, and an infant mortality rate nearly seven times, the Canadian average.[21] Moreover, as some of the older illnesses are brought under control, others take their place. Venereal disease and alcoholism are widespread.

Other diseases related to white culture include obesity, high cholesterol levels, gall bladder ailments, heart disease, and poor dental conditions.

After World War II, the Department of Health and Welfare began constructing Arctic nursing stations, each staffed by one or two nurses. Almost every village has one now. The stations contain a few beds and are sufficiently equipped to render emergency service for patients awaiting transfer to a hospital. By 1969, medical facilities in the far North included 34 out-patient clinics, 85 health centres, 47 nursing stations, and 14 public hospitals.[22] In addition, six surplus military hospitals have been redesignated for use by Inuit patients. Some contracting-out with private agencies for medical services has also occurred, one example being the ten-year agreement with the International Grenfell Association in Newfoundland.

In the attack against tuberculosis, the practice was adopted of flying patients to medical centres in Edmonton and Quebec City. Such transfers from the Arctic to the south are not without attendant problems. Years spent in warm, relatively comfortable hospitals with little exercise, constant cleanliness, and prepared foods make it difficult for the ex-patients to fit back into northern life.

Medical services for the Inuit are continuing to improve. Plans are afoot for an extensive program of hospital insurance to cover all northern native people. While criticisms do occur of some government programs, particularly the sending of patients to southern cities for treatment, the fact remains that Inuit health has improved remarkably since the end of World War II. The 600 patients in tuberculosis centres in 1956, for example, were reduced to only 350 by 1962.

A Cross-National Assessment

Canada's Inuit have recently made considerable progress in areas such as health and education where they used to be greatly disadvantaged. They have also proved their ability once more to roll with the pitch-and-toss of change. Some beneficial programs, though, like the housing scheme of 1966 and the establishment of a Baffin Island National Park in 1972, have elicited hostile responses from many Inuit, because the government did its planning and deciding without any prior consultation of those most affected.

Slowly, northern people have begun to organize themselves politically. They no longer simply rely on the Canadian Association in Support of Native People (formerly the Indian-Eskimo Association), which consists of outsiders interested in protecting native interests; they have begun to look after themselves more. Because of the growing concern in southern Canada with questions of environment, minority rights, and social issues, native organizations are now receiving support from citizens' groups and from provincial and federal governments. During the Berger Inquiry into the impact of the Mackenzie Valley Pipeline on the northern environment, Inuit from many communities spoke out effectively and often movingly about the potential destruction of wildlife and traditional cultural patterns that is likely to occur with industrial expansion in the North. Each province and territory now has an association of registered Indians and another of non-status Indians and Métis. There are also national bodies, the National Indian Brotherhood and the Native Council of Canada for Indians, and the Inuit Tapirisat of Canada for Inuit, all of them based in Ottawa. Even so, the Inuit would obviously benefit from stronger central leadership.

Despite improvements, Canada's treatment of its Inuit compares unfavourably with that of Denmark, the United States, and the Soviet Union. The Danes have not operated a system of police outposts in Greenland, despite there being more Inuit there than in Canada. In 1939, Canada spent $119,000 on the RCMP in the Arctic and only $58,000 in Inuit health and welfare. In Greenland, no expenditures for police occurred, while more than one-third of a million dollars was earmarked for Inuit health and welfare.[23]

The Danish administrative and economic attitude toward Greenland and its Inuit population has been characterized as "protective and non-exploitative."[24] Not only have death rates and disease been markedly reduced, but the Danes also have supported the maintenance of Inuit culture in all areas except religion. Greenland schools are staffed by Inuit teachers, with instruction and textbooks in the native language. The idea was to help people live better where they were by utilizing local resources and techniques proven by experience rather than forcing people to migrate endlessly in a quest for survival. Illiteracy was abolished in Greenland over a century ago, the clergy are native sons, and leadership in government is vested in the native population.

Greenland's Inuit exhibit little desire to immigrate to Denmark or elsewhere. After considerable experience at the local level, they now govern the entire island though their own elected parliament. In addition, from 1955 onward, Danish instructors have taught technological courses in order to prepare Greenlanders for coming industrialization. Such training, along with a growing bilingualism, will enable the Inuit of Greenland to take advantage of opportunities in the modern world.

Reports from eastern Siberia indicate that the Soviet Union has provided well for its Inuit population. Government hospitals and community centres have been operating for many years. Educational levels are high, some Soviet Inuit even pilot aircraft, and most live in well-insulated, prefabricated houses equipped with electric power.

The United States land settlement with the "Eskimos" of Alaska is of tremendous potential importance for Canada's Inuit. Exploration for Alaskan gas and oil and the eventual need for pipeline construction gave rise to a movement by native people, supported by many other Americans, that resulted in the Alaska Native Claims Settlement Act of 1971.

The 55,000 Eskimos of Alaska were compensated for the government's taking of their lands. All Alaskan-born United States citizens of at least one-quarter Eskimo, Aleut, or Indian blood, born on or before December 18, 1971, are entitled to share in the settlement, including some now living in Canada.

The settlement involves recognizing that the native peoples of Alaska fully own forty million acres of land, to be selected by them. In addition, they are awarded $962.5 million in cash and royalties as compensation for past losses. Most of the money will go into development funds controlled by regional native corporations.

The Alaskan outcome has quickened the desire of Canada's Inuit to seek similar redress from the courts and legislative assemblies. But if the Nishga case of 1967, in which the Nishga Indians tried unsuccessfully to claim title to certain land in British Columbia, is representative, Canadian courts are anxious to avoid assuming the governmental lead in granting claims of native people for lands taken in or outside of treaty agreements. Even so, the Inuit have submitted land claims in 1976 to 750,000 square miles of land and 800,000 square miles of water in an area north of the tree line to be called Nanavut (Our Land). The Inuit Tapirisat of Canada represents these claims in Ottawa, and an Inuit Development Corporation has been established to deal with their economic and financial ramifications.

An equitable decision is no trivial matter. The Arctic has been transformed from a frozen wasteland into a military front line and now into a potential treasure house. Perhaps the prophetic words of Peter Freuchen may become true:

> Far from being discouraged at the changes I see and yearning for a return to times that are past, I look forward to the day when the Arctic will help man to realize his dream of making the earth a better and more happy place in which to live. [25]

If so, the Inuit, rooted in the area, would rightfully be among the first beneficiaries.

NOTES

[1] *Canada Year Book 1974*, Statistics Canada (Ottawa: Information Canada, 1974), p. 167.

[2] Van Den Steenhoven, Geert, "The Law Through Eskimo Eyes," in Van Steensel, Maja, ed., *People of Light and Dark* (Ottawa: Information Canada, 1974), p. 92.

[3] *Re Eskimos* (1939) S.C.R. 104.

[4] Cited in Jenness, Diamond, *Eskimo Administration II*, Canada (Montreal: Arctic Institute of North America, Technical Paper No. 14, May 1964), p. 54.

[5] Jenness, *op. cit.*, p. 46.

[6] *Ibid.*, p. 42.

[7] Van Den Steenhoven, Geert, *Leadership and Law Among the Eskimos of the Keewatin District, Northwest Territories* (Rijswijk, Holland, 1959), p. 131.

[8] Vallee, Frank G., *Kabloona and Eskimo* (Ottawa: St. Paul University, 1967), p. 156.

[9] *Ibid.*

[10] Rowley, Graham, "But Change Confronts the Eskimo," in Smith, I. Norman, ed., *The Unbelievable Land* (Ottawa: Information Canada, 1974), p. 12. A third language, Aleut, is spoken by ethnically related natives of Alaska's island chain.

[11] Hobart, Charles W., "Eskimo Education in the Canadian Arctic," *Canadian Review of Sociology and Anthropology*, 7:1, February 1970, p. 54.

[12] Crowe, Keith J., *A History of the Original Peoples of Northern Canada* (Montreal: Arctic Institute of North America, 1974), p. 168.

[13] Jenness, *op. cit.*, pp. 75-76.

[14] Crowe, *op. cit.*, p. 175.

[15] *Ordinances of the N.W.T., 1966, 2nd Session*, Chapter 5 (1966).

[16] Crowe, *op. cit.*, p. 192.

[17] Vallee, Frank, "The Co-operative Movement in the North", in Van Steensel, Maja, ed., *People of Light and Dark* (Ottawa: Information Canada, 1974), p. 46.

[18] Crowe, *op. cit.*, p. 186.

[19] Stevenson, D. S., *Problems of Eskimo Relocation for Industrial Employment* (Ottawa: Department of Indian Affairs and Northern Development, 1968). p. 6.

[20] Jenness, *op. cit.*, p. 83.

[21] "Arctic Housing," *North*, 16:1, January-February 1969, p. 9.

[22] Jenness, *op. cit.*, p. 32.

[23] *Ibid.*, p. 71.

[24] Hobart, C. W., and C. S. Brant, "Eskimo Education, Danish and Canadian: A Comparison", *Canadian Review of Sociology and Anthropology*, 3:2, May, 1966, p. 48.

[25] Freuchen, D., *Peter Freuchen's Book of the Eskimos* (New York: The World Publishing Co., 1961), p. 441.

Chapter 4

BLACKS

Blacks have lived in Canada since 1628. Despite comprising a visibly distinct minority, their numbers have always been in doubt because of gaps or errors in official counts. The census for 1971 suggests a figure of 62,470, or about 0.4 percent of Canada's total population, while estimates in the press and in magazines run as high as 250,000.[1]

The obscurity of the Canadian Black situation can be traced, in part, to the lack of a pervasive Canadian Black identity. Blacks from Nova Scotia to British Columbia have never joined in a common cause or organization or under a common leader. True, a Canadian Association for the Advancement of Coloured People does exist, but it has little communication with its American counterpart. Moreover, it is not to the national association but to churches and to the Canadian Labour Congress that the Nova Scotia Association for the Advancement of Coloured People primarily looks for guidance. The National Black Coalition, established in Toronto in 1969, also has yet to make the influence of Blacks felt in Canadian society. There is presently in Canada no Black national leader with the stature of a Martin Luther King. Nor have competent Black administrators in national labour organizations, like A. R. Blanchette of the Brotherhood of Sleeping Car Porters, been able to rally Canada's Blacks. Each Black community has its own, often able, spokesman; but these persons are little known nationally. And without such unifying leadership, the Canadian Black remains voiceless.

We cannot claim to speak for Canada's Black population, but we can briefly articulate some of the experiences and problems it has met through the centuries. The rather complex pattern of immigration will be discussed first, and then the practice of slavery. Thereafter, attention will focus upon more recent discrimination against, and disabilities of, Blacks in education, employment, housing, and public accommodations. A general commentary on the current situation of Blacks in Canada, particularly as compared to that of their American counterparts, concludes the chapter.

Immigration

Until the significant West Indian immigration of the past fifteen years, virtually all Canadian Blacks had entered Canada from the United States. First to arrive in any considerable numbers were slaves brought to Nova Scotia in the late 1750s by former New England residents after the expulsion of the Acadians. When the American Revolution broke out in 1776, there were already some five hundred slaves in Nova Scotia, and the figure was to triple as white Loyalists, who supported the British, fled the American colonies during and immediately after the American Revolutionary War (1776-1781), bringing their slaves with them.[2] In addition, three thousand Blacks, who had been emancipated in the American colonies by the British in order to both weaken the South and obtain labourers for the British forces, entered Canada between April 15 and November 30, 1783. Most of these freed men found their way to Nova Scotia aboard ships from New York, after arrangements had been made between Sir Guy Carleton, commander of the British troops in North America, and General Washington.

Besides permitting slavery, from the start Nova Scotia discriminated against Blacks in other ways. When the first group of free Black Loyalists arrived there from Boston in 1776, the suggestion was made that they be used as ransom for British prisoners held by the Americans.[3] Furthermore, while free Blacks had been promised treatment equal to that of their white peers, the British pledge of one hundred-acre grants of land to each Black failed to materialize. Most Blacks received no land at all; if anything was given them it was mainly barren one-acre lots on the edge of white Loyalist townships, where they were segregated from the main population.

Certainly, in every instance where acreage was granted to both Black and white settlers, Blacks received less. For example, while Blacks were given one-acre lots in Digby, whites were granted from one-hundred to four-hundred-acre lots throughout Annapolis County. Moreover, only Blacks who settled on Chedabucto Bay or in Preston township were not completely segregated.[4] Most of the Black settlements eventually failed; as a result many former American slaves, now freed in Canada, continued to work as hired or indentured servants. (The system of indenture, or apprenticeship, as it was sometimes called, had existed in Nova Scotia long before the arrival of the Black Loyalists, and it differed little from outright slavery.)

The British were also supposed to supply all Loyalists with food and provisions for three years, or until they could survive on their own. However, the new Black arrivals fared as badly with food as they had with land. The economy of Nova Scotia failed to develop as planned, and to make matters worse, by 1789 a serious famine was confronting all of British North America. The hijacking of a supply ship in 1788 meant that no government food at all arrived in Guysborough County; had it not been for the charity of church organizations and people in England, hundreds of Blacks would have died of starvation.[5]

The Black Loyalists were never truly secure. They were deprived of such rights of British subjects as trial by jury, and they lived in constant fear. From 1785 to 1791, no white in Guysborough County suffered corporal punishment, but during this same period Blacks were whipped for stealing food and one Black woman was hanged for stealing a bundle of used clothes. In Halifax in 1785, three Black men were hanged, one of them for the theft of a bag of potatoes.[6]

Some Loyalists subsequently moved from Nova Scotia into the other two Maritime provinces, New Brunswick and Prince Edward Island, bringing their slaves with them. There is no way of knowing how many of the several thousand Blacks in the Maritimes were slaves and how many were free. Clearly, however, Blacks in Nova Scotia had become so disillusioned by 1792 that twelve hundred of them accepted an offer by the Sierra Leone Company and sailed to Africa. With the British government underwriting the cost of the emigration plan, passage was provided free to Blacks seeking to return to their "homeland."

An interesting and colourful group of Blacks entered Nova Scotia in 1796. Some five hundred and fifty Maroons, descendants of fugitive West Indian slaves of the seventeenth and eighteenth centuries, were deported from Jamaica and settled in the Preston area on lands vacated by those Blacks who had gone to Africa. In 1800, though, the entire Maroon colony itself was shipped under military escort to Sierra Leone.

The exodus of such large numbers of Blacks had economic repercussions: trade was depressed by the loss of Black consumers; a reserve of cheap labour was no longer available; settlements such as Preston, Birchtown, and Brindley Town were largely deserted and their tax revenues ceased. Even more important was the social dislocation caused by the exodus. Most of the Black teachers, preachers, and community leaders were gone. Instead of aiding in the development of a distinct and separate community of Blacks in Canada, the Black Loyalists contributed immensely to the growth of Sierra Leone.

A second major influx of American Blacks entered Canada in 1815. During the War of 1812, Britain offered freedom to every American-owned slave who would desert his master and join the British. Some thirty-six hundred former slaves were thereby brought by British ships into Canadian ports, with nearly two thousand taken to Nova Scotia. These "Refugee Blacks" were housed temporarily on Melville Island, site of a prisoner-of-war camp, pending their transfer to other parts of the province. Most were then sent to the depopulated and deserted towns of the Black Loyalists, where they too were unable to support themselves on the small plots of marginal land.

As it happened, the Refugee Blacks entered the country at the worst of times. There was high unemployment, among both Blacks and Whites. To make matters worse, 1815 became known as the "Year of the Mice," since entire fields of grain and potatoes were destroyed by these rodents; while 1816 was the "Year Without a Summer," in which entire crops were destroyed by a heavy frost and a ten-inch snowfall in June. Attempts were made to encourage Blacks to move to Trinidad, but only 93 accepted. Most Nova Scotia Blacks today are descendants of the Refugee Blacks.

The period 1815-1861 gave rise to the so-called "Negro question." When the Blacks could no longer support themselves on marginal farms and small villages, they migrated into the larger cities where their numbers attracted the attention and hostility of officials and the general Nova Scotian population as never before. The descendants of Loyalist and Refugee Blacks merged, forming a new community devoid of the Loyalist tradition.

Despite these trends, Blacks from the United States saw Canada as a bulwark not only against slavery but also against prejudice and discrimination. They travelled as individuals and in groups along the route of the "Underground Railroad," which terminated at Amherstburg, formerly Fort Malden, on the Detroit River. By the late 1820s, Blacks were slipping into Canada in substantial numbers. With the passage of the Fugitive Slave Act in 1850, the flow became a flood, for now even the northern states were no longer safe havens for runaway and freed Blacks.

As the number of fugitives increased, so too did levels of prejudice among white Canadians and even opposition from Canadian Blacks. The American Blacks were uninterested in returning to Africa; they wished to remain in North America. They also gave every indication that their stay in Canada was only temporary and that they planned to re-enter the United States, perhaps by force. Some whites saw this as the purpose of the British-American Institute, better known as "Dawn," built on a two-hundred-acre tract near Chatham, Ontario. The real purpose of the school, in fact, was to provide an opportunity for Blacks to take manual training courses. Similar deductions were drawn from the fact that most of the American fugitives stopped just beyond the Canadian border, clustering at Amherstburg and along the Niagara frontier.

While no official figures are available on the number of fugitive slaves crossing into Canada prior to 1861, it has been estimated that as many as thirty a day would cross the Detroit River at Fort Malden alone.[7] Between 1850 and 1860, perhaps twenty thousand Blacks entered Canada, in effect doubling its Black population. Attempts to recover American fugitives were occasionally made by American owners under the provisions of the Webster-Ashburton Treaty of 1842, but these attempts habitually failed. Once the American Civil War began, however, the American Blacks began recrossing the border of their own volition; by the end of the war most of the fugitives had returned to the United States.

While most Blacks have entered eastern Canada (primarily Nova Scotia, Ontario, and Quebec), Blacks from California and other American western states focused upon British Columbia. California had begun placing restrictions on Blacks in 1850 by disqualifying them from giving evidence against white persons. In 1852, legislation was enacted which would have allowed newly arriving slaveowners to retain their property, despite the 1849 State Constitution's prohibition against slavery. In January 1858, the governor of California ridiculed abolitionist activities; the following month, the San Francisco Board of Education ordered all Black children to attend special schools; and one month after that, the State legislature debated a bill that would restrict immigration of Blacks and impose mandatory registration on them.[8] As a consequence, Blacks from San Francisco met in April to consider emigration. They decided upon Vancouver Island. A delegation travelled there, and after being assured that Blacks would be accepted as settlers without legal discrimination, purchased land for a colony.

The Blacks who arrived in British Columbia from California, and from more distant Oklahoma and Kansas, were not fugitives. They intended to live permanently in Canada. Skilled and literate, they were accepted by Victoria's white population. Many of the Blacks went into business for themselves; others worked for the Hudson's Bay Company.

This British Columbia venture marked the closest approximation to equality for Canadian Blacks in the nineteenth century. Despite many instances of prejudice, Blacks in Victoria were not barred from public schools or from holding public office of from membership in churches, as they were for some time in Ontario and Nova Scotia. One factor that lay behind the Blacks' success in British Columbia may have been that some moved to the interior of Vancouver Island or to the mainland, so that their numbers were less obvious than in cities of eastern Canada.

In October 1909, Blacks from Oklahoma arrived in Saskatchewan at the invitation of the railroads and the prairie governments. They had been promised good farm lands, but on arriving had to accept inferior allotments. Black settlements in this region failed to grow, however, mainly because the Canadian government prevented additional groups of Oklahoma Blacks from entering these provinces. Indeed, when attempts to turn them back failed at border and customs check points, a special medical officer was sent to Emerson, Manitoba to examine the Black settlers already in Canada and determine whether the climate was too severe for them. An investigation in April 1911 revealed that the Commissioner of Immigration for Western Canada had offered a fee to the medical inspector at Emerson for every Black he rejected.[9]

Suddenly, "climate" became a leading issue for those opposing the immigration of Blacks. Legal justification for such a restrictive policy lay in one of the original enabling clauses of the Immigration Act which allowed the making of regulations.

. . . to prohibit the admission of persons by reason of (1) nationality, citizenship, ethnic group, occupation . . . (or) unsuitability having regard to the climatic, economic, social . . . condition . . . in the area or country from or through which such person comes to Canada.[10]

A half-century later, in 1952, W. E. Harris, Minister of Citizenship and Immigration, reached much the same conclusion about "climate":

One of the conditions for admission to Canada is that immigrants should be able to readily become adapted and integrated into the life of the community within a reasonable time after their entry. In the light of experience it would be unrealistic to say that immigrants who have spent the greater part of their life in tropical or semi-tropical countries become readily adapted to the Canadian mode of life which, to no small extent, is determined by climatic conditions. It is a matter of record that natives of such countries are more apt to break down in health than immigrants from countries where the climate is more akin to that of Canada.[11]

In fact, this is hardly "a matter of record" at all. Canada, to be sure, is a northern country, but there are parts of the United States with colder weather than parts of southern Canada. Thousands of immigrants from tropical countries have lived in northern American cities for years with no "breakdown in health." When the Alcan Highway was built from Dawson creek, British Columbia to Big Delta, Alaska as a joint project of Canadian and American forces during World War II, nearly a third of the labourers on the project were American Blacks.[12]

During the early years of this century, problems about the admission of Blacks into Canada severely strained an already precarious Canadian-American relationship. The Dominion Commissioner of Immigration in Winnipeg, J. Bruce Walker, admitted that the Canadian government "was doing all in its power through a policy of persuasion, to keep negroes out of Western Canada." Walker admitted that, ". . . it was his purpose to bar [Blacks] from Canada, upon the broad ground of being undesirables."[13] The immigration authorities in Winnipeg wanted American railroads, such as the Rock Island and the Southern Pacific, to reduce somehow Canada's attractiveness to Blacks in their advertisements, while at the same time enhancing it for white Americans. In February 1912, the Great Northern Railway sent notices to its employees that Blacks would not be admitted to Canada under any circumstances and that ticket sales to them for journeys between St. Paul, Minnesota and the Canadian border were to be discouraged. Restrictions on Black immigration were later extended to include visits by Blacks to Canada, since "visitors" might attempt to remain permanently in the country.

The outbreak of World War I put an end to any need for persistent Canadian efforts against Black admission, for by 1914 Blacks had begun moving increasingly into northern American cities, and their interest in immigrating to Canada waned. Indeed, not until the late 1960s did Canada experience another major influx of Blacks, this time not from the United States but from the West Indies. Because of the British influence on Canada, recent Black immigration from the (Commonwealth) West Indies has far exceeded that from Africa or the United States. By 1970, in fact, the West Indies was the third largest regional source of immigrants to Canada. No accurate figures are available, because of illegal immigration, losses due to emigration, and the usual census inadequacies, but it has been estimated that the present West Indian population in Canada actually exceeds one hundred thousand. Most live in Ontario, principally in the Toronto area.

The majority of West Indian immigrants have been women, because of the availability of domestic work in cities and the relative ease with which female domestics are able to find white Canadian sponsors. Even as early as the 1920s the Canadian government made exceptions to its otherwise exclusionist immigration laws in order to allow the entrance of West Indian female domestics. In 1955, the Canadian West Indian Female Domestic Scheme gave formal, if limited, recognition to domestics as a special occupational group warranting exception to prevailing immigration rules. The Scheme remained in effect until 1967 when it was replaced by a more liberalized set of general immigration regulations. One may perhaps get some idea of the scope of female immigration into Canada from the West Indies by noting that between 1946 and 1973, 448 persons, all women, entered from the island of Montserrat alone.[14]

Slavery

Slavery was never as strong an institution in Canada as in the United States. Under the French, slavery was less a matter of doctrine than a product of circumstance and accident. Nor did the Catholic Church actively support slavery, though it did not actively oppose it. Slavery did not gain a firm grip in Canada because it tends to meet the needs of a plantation system of agriculture: one-crop, mass-production, gang-labour. In addition, the French were relatively unenthusiastic about slave labour. They felt that it did not pay, that free labour was more productive.

Nonetheless, slavery was given a legal formulation in New France between 1689 and 1709.[15] The *Code Noir*, promulgated in 1685 for the West Indies, was also used as customary law in New France, though not officially proclaimed there. The *Code* was drafted to protect the white man from slaves' theft, revolt, and escape. By 1759, there were about four thousand slaves in New France, both Indian *panis* and Black.

With the Treaty of Paris in 1763, France ceded the whole of its North American territory east of the Mississippi River to Great Britain. One side effect of this was to strengthen the institution of slavery legally and religiously. Not only did British officials and Protestant sects support slavery, but governmental authorities encouraged the immigration of slaveowners (like the New England Loyalists) and their slaves into the country. Black slaves soon supplanted the *panis,* and for a while slavery was on the increase in Canada.

In general, British legislation on the subject was harsher than French, though the institution would in fact soon begin to wane and within another generation be abolished. One sign of the waning was the fact that after a couple of decades the Loyalists decided to free their own slaves, for economic reasons. A harbinger of the impending abolition was provided by an Upper Canada statute confirming the ownership of slaves held as of 1793, while at the same time stipulating that no new slaves could be brought into the province and that persons subsequently born into slavery there would be freed upon reaching the age of twenty-five.[16] Moreover, in Nova Scotia, where slavery existed in practice though not in law, attempts in 1787 and again in 1808 to give it legal status failed. Legalized slavery finally ended throughout the British Empire with the passage of the Emancipation Act of 1833 by the British Parliament.[17]

Abolition created no major problems for Canada. Regional economies were little affected. Since 1833, Blacks who were Canadian citizens have enjoyed many legal rights and privileges on par with other Canadians. Unlike some minorities discussed in this book, they have always been able to vote in both federal and provincial elections. Their standing in courts of law has almost always been the same as that of other Canadian citizens. (One exception: in British Columbia Blacks for a long time could not serve on juries.) Their consumption of liquor has not been questioned or restricted. Yet Blacks have experienced racially based discrimination in education, employment, housing, and public accommodations. Moreover, much of this discrimination has occurred not merely in practice, but under the protection of law.

Education

Even during their early years in Nova Scotia, Blacks did not enjoy educational opportunities equal to those of other Nova Scotians. Indeed, Winks argues that historically, Black school children have met more hostility in Nova Scotia than in other regions of Canada.[18] The first schools for them in Nova Scotia and New Brunswick were church-related, run by groups like the Society for the Propagation of the Gospel. Emphasis was placed on religious instruction rather than on the development of skills which might have led to social and economic betterment. Teachers were often poorly trained and underpaid.

By the 1850s, segregated public schools could be found operating in both Nova Scotia and Ontario. Segregated schools had been legalized throughout the Province of Canada in 1849 by a statute that permitted municipal councils to establish separate schools for Blacks.[19] The practice was reinforced by the Separate Schools Act of 1859, which provided that any five Black families could petition local school officials to establish schools for Blacks.[20] Ostensibly the Separate Schools Act was a voluntary procedural device, but its practical effect was to create a system that could force all Black children out of white local schools. *De facto* residential segregation was thus transformed into *de jure*, educational segregation.

In many localities, private church schools for Blacks continued to exist alongside the public (segregated) school system: for example, those in Halifax, Preston, Digby, and Shelburne, Nova Scotia lasted well into the twentieth century. Indeed, few Nova Scotian Blacks were being educated in public schools at all.[21] In addition, segregation of the public schools itself became a major issue in Halifax, and spilled over into the Legislative Assembly, where the existence of legally sanctioned discrimination was pointed up:

> A petition of George Davis and others, was presented by Mr. Harrington, and read, setting forth that they are coloured citizens and ratepayers of the City of Halifax, that by a minute of the Council of Public Instruction passed in December, 1876, all coloured children were from thenceforth excluded from the Common Schools, and separate schools were established for their use, which are of an inferior grade, and in which they do not receive equal advantages with children attending the Common Schools; for which and other reasons, as detailed in the petition, they pray that such minutes of Council be repealed.[22]

Although proponents of segregated schools prevailed, an amendment was passed by the Legislative Assembly declaring that:

> . . . coloured pupils could not be excluded from instruction in the section or ward in which they lived. The government could continue to establish separate schools for both sexes and for colours, although if no Negro school existed admission to the public school was to be guaranteed.[23]

Note, however, that the amendment affected segregated schooling only in those areas where Black schools did not exist or where the number of Black children was considered insufficient to justify the expense of a separate school.

As revised in 1918, Nova Scotia's Education Act still allowed school inspectors to recommend separate facilities for different races, although it also emphasized that Black students could not be excluded from the public schools. Not until 1954, in fact, was reference to race finally deleted from the statute.[24] Well into the postwar period, educational opportunities for Nova Scotia's Blacks remained grossly inadequate. Black teachers in the usually dilapidated separate schools were both poorly qualified and underpaid. Student attendance was irregular, and at times even the schools themselves operated intermittently. In the Lincolnville area of Guysborough County, Nova Scotia the schoolhouse burned down in the last decade of the nineteenth century and was not replaced until about 1930.[25]

Court decisions often buttressed the system of segregated schools. In 1861, a court upheld the total exclusion of Blacks in Chatham, Ontario, from ordinary public schools. Instead, they could legally be assigned to one or another of two segregated schools, regardless of the distance from home. In 1884, another court ruled against the transfer of Black children from a Black to a white public school, or their direct enrollment in a white school, on the grounds that there was insufficient room in the white school. [26]

Only in the rarest circumstances was a Black able to win in court. One such example involved the case of *Washington v. Trustees of Charlotteville* (1854), in which attempts to gerrymander school district boundaries were struck down. [27] After three trials, the Black plaintiff from Simcoe won a verdict for damages and costs in an action against school trustees for barring his child from the local school. The school board, however, had no property that could be sold. The parent consequently had to pay his own court costs, and was forced to sell his farm in order to do so. The possibility that a judicial victory might turn out to be so resoundingly hollow was a strong deterrent to Blacks seeking relief through the courts.

After 1910, separate Black schools began to disappear in Ontario through a lack of students and a more enlightened and tolerant attitude on the part of the white community. Still, it took until 1965 for the last Black school in Ontario to close its doors. Legally segregated education ended in Nova Scotia in 1963, although some schools that are completely Black, since they serve an all-Black rural community, can be found in Nova Scotia today.

At the higher education level, qualified Blacks had been admitted on a basis of equality to the University of Toronto and Queen's University even before the American Civil War, and by the end of the nineteenth century Blacks had also attended most Maritime universities. The numbers involved, then and now, have been quite small, however. One factor that militates against Blacks moving on to university is their high dropout rate in elementary school. Throughout the 1960s, for example, most Nova Scotian Blacks left school at the end of the sixth or seventh grade. Moreover, those Halifax Blacks who, as of 1969, did remain in school were considerably older for each grade, on average, than white children.

In any event, one may entertain doubts about the immediate effectiveness of schools in breaking down the barriers that have separated Black from white. Despite improved teaching standards, more sympathetic governmental agencies, the elimination of separate schools, and a growing concern among Blacks, educational processes need time if they are to help bring about long overdue changes in a society. As Winks noted in 1969:

. . . the present Negro generation in Nova Scotia could not be liberated in any case. The cycle of poverty, ignorance, and unemployment had lasted far too long for anyone but the most idealistic to expect the Nova Scotian Negro to assimilate to Nova Scotian society quickly or easily, or for the Nova Scotian white, however much he might be prepared to concede the Negroes' inherent equality, to think of them as equal in fact as well as in potential. For Negroes were not yet equal in fact and were unlikely to be until the slow curative powers of equal education had made their impact. It was not this generation that had been liberated but the next.[28]

Recent studies of school systems in Toronto and elsewhere point up evidence of continuing racial discrimination against Blacks. Until a few years ago, textbooks paid no attention at all to the historical background and present-day culture of Canadian Blacks.[29] Racial stereotyping is also frequently apparent. Many misguided teachers have lower expectations of Black students, considering them to be slow learners incapable of high achievement. Not surprisingly, many Black youngsters have developed negative attitudes about school. Inadequate counselling and advising have resulted in considerable "streaming," whereby Black students are channelled into trade schools and vocational classes rather than academic studies.[30]

Even when highly motivated and encouraged by their parents, many Black children, because of relocation and encirclement by a strange culture, can easily become isolated and under emotional strain in school. This in turn may lead to behaviour problems, and to a high dropout rate.

While there have been growing numbers of racial incidents in the public schools of larger metropolitan areas, efforts are being made to correct the situation. In Toronto, for example, a Black Education Project has been developed to help students adjust and succeed in the schools. Teachers are also being encouraged to familiarize themselves with the history and current conditions of Blacks. A Commonwealth Teacher Exchange Program is available whereby Canadian teachers may study the cultural backgrounds of children who immigrate to Canada. Some community agencies have been proving helpful, too. For example, the Harriet Tubman Centre in Toronto, sponsored by the YMCA, services West Indian youths in the area.[31]

Employment

If any occupational category can be described as "characteristic" or typical for Blacks, it is service. When slavery existed, Canadian Blacks habitually worked as household servants. To be sure, the Refugee Blacks from the War of 1812 often became farm labourers, and many of the Black Loyalists were skilled tradesmen. The building of railroads saw Blacks working on construction gangs. But as additional immigrants from Europe went into agriculture and construction work on transcontinental railroads, in many instances the Blacks were displaced.

More recently, too, Blacks have occupied the lowest rungs of the urban employment ladder. In 1941, almost half the employed Black males of Montreal were railway porters, while four-fifths of the employed Black females were domestics.[32] In Nova Scotia, employment opportunities for Blacks are the least satisfactory in all Canada.

The employment experiences of West Indian women show, however, that the situation is becoming somewhat more fluid. Most of these women enter Canada with a lower-class background, and speak a dialect of English. Most are sponsored by white Canadians for work as domestics and hence have employment awaiting them. Others arrive via a "broker" who is able to locate potential immigrants and place them in jobs. (The services of the "broker" may be paid for by either the employer or the immigrant.) Still others come as visitors, and then solicit friends or possibly employers to obtain landed immigrant status.

While the West Indian women have little difficulty in securing jobs as domestics, most leave them at the earliest opportunity. Upward mobility from domestic work, however, is not easy; often it depends upon the woman's ability to "make friends" with people for whom she works or with West Indians who have been resident for some time in Canada. Domestics typically move into blue-collar jobs through acquaintances, the Canadian Manpower Training Program, or advertisements in newspapers. Transfer to white-collar positions is more difficult, and usually requires more education or some vocational training, but West Indians are ambitious to upgrade themselves. Studies of West Indian women indicate that some have assumed considerable responsibility and worked to enhance their skills even without government aid.[33] While substantial numbers of these women have found work as nurses and nursing aides and in the civil service, for many others life remains difficult, lonely, and isolated.[34]

Considerable movement can also be seen among West Indian immigrants generally. Their principal reason for emigrating to Canada, in fact, has been to take advantage of better economic opportunities. Admittedly, some suffer an initial downward shift in status by being unable to obtain new positions comparable to those they held in the Caribbean. Such an immediate decline, however, is a phenomenon often experienced by immigrants of various ethnic and racial backgrounds. Once they have secured further experience and improved their qualifications by additional educational or vocational training, most West Indians are able to compete successfully in the Canadian job market.

West Indian white-collar workers are apparently more successful than blue-collar workers in fulfilling their occupational aspirations. One difficulty facing blue-collar workers is that they are often not readily accepted by their trade union licensing bodies.[35] As one would expect, the longer an immigrant remains in Canada, the greater his chances of obtaining employment in his preferred occupation. Economic achievement—i.e., family income—is also conditioned by educational level and skin tone. Far more light-skinned Blacks earn more than the national median income than do the dark-skinned.[36] Since levels of colour and education are interrelated, the effect is considerably increased.

The initial downward mobility and status dislocation of the West Indians' first years in Canada gradually turn around. By their seventh year of residence, most have in fact improved upon the position they had prior to entering the country. Educational and vocational training enables them to compensate for the disadvantages of colour. Indeed, despite discrimination in employment, the majority of West Indians view their new economic conditions as superior to what they left in the Caribbean.

Changes can also be noted in the acceptance of Blacks into the labour movement. In the summer of 1918, for example, the Black porters of the Canadian National Railway organized a union, the Order of Sleeping Car Porters, and applied to the Trades and Labour Congress for a charter. That application was rejected. It was another year before the Brotherhood of Railway Workers agreed to strike a racial qualification (which restricted membership to whites) from its constitution, thereby allowing the Sleeping Car Porters to join the Brotherhood. This was the first time a Canadian union had abolished racial restrictions on membership.

By contrast, from World War II onward labour unions were in the forefront of the anti-discrimination fight. Pressures from the railway unions upon the Ontario Legislature resulted in the passage of the Racial Discrimination Act of 1944, which prohibited the publication or display of any symbol, sign, or notice that expressed racial or religious discrimination. Similar pressure by the unions in 1950 resulted in the passage of Ontario's Fair Employment Practices Act.

Governmental and private efforts have both been directed of late toward discriminatory practices in employment. The federal government, most of the provinces, and the Northwest Territories have passed Fair Employment Practices Acts. At the provincial level, organized labour has become increasingly active in promoting equal employment opportunities for all minority groups, including the Blacks. The Winnipeg Joint Labour Committee to Combat Racial Intolerance, established in 1946, has become a model for such committees elsewhere. The development of Human Rights Commissions has also proved beneficial to labour because of their investigative powers and because of the publicity they are able to generate about discriminatory conditions. No employer relishes adverse comment; this proves a strong deterrent to unethical labour practices. Nevertheless, the Ontario Human Rights Commission reports more complaints of unfair employment practices from Blacks than from any other group. In particular, many younger Blacks feel that they are habitually last hired and first fired.

Generally, job discrimination met by Blacks can be broken down into two broad categories. One involves application and hiring. The other concerns employment conditions: for example, work assignments and denial of promotion. A federal government survey of "Black Workers in the Civil Service" shows that Blacks in Nova Scotia are systematically discriminated against at all levels of employment.[37] And the problems are certainly not limited to either that province or to government service.

Housing

At the time of the Loyalists, Black servants lived on the property of their masters, occasionally in the same house. Later, communal living was attempted in the so-called model towns or settlements established in southern Ontario by fugitive slaves from the United States. The best known of these all-Black communities was Dawn Settlement, found by Josiah Henson, a runaway slave, and Henry Bibb, editor of *The Voice of the Fugitive*, published in Windsor. At its peak, Dawn contained about a hundred families living on some three hundred acres of land. Other colonies were located in nearby areas of Ontario: the Refugees' Home Settlement near Windsor, the Mount Hope Settlement near Caledonia, the Wilberforce Settlement near London, and the Elgin Association Settlement (also known as the Buxton Settlement) in Kent County. Most had a somewhat utopian flavour and lasted only until their inhabitants returned to the United States after the American Civil War.

In Nova Scotia, where Blacks are poorer than whites and whites poorer than most Canadians elsewhere, many Blacks live in rural areas. Their houses are usually substandard, some little more than shanties that lack a bare minimum of heating and plumbing. For the most part, however, Canadian Blacks live in cities.

The 1971 Census indicates that 9,380 Blacks (4,770 "Negroes" and 4,610 West Indians) were living in Montreal, and 27,000 Blacks (12,000 "Negroes" and 15,000 West Indians) in Toronto. These figures undoubtedly are low. The Ontario Human Rights Commission has stated with respect to the Black population of Toronto:

> . . . it is probable that the black population was not adequately enumerated, largely because many individuals who may have entered the country as visitors and then remained, did not want to be counted.
>
> A second reason is a structural one; the Canadian government does not inquire into the racial background of the population. . . . Frequently West Indians come to Canada via Great Britain, other West Indians are classified as East Indians, Chinese, etc. and would not be counted as 'black'. In short, many of the problems of enumeration noted by observers in the 19th century are still operative.

The present (1975) black population of Metropolitan Toronto, including the immigrants who have arrived since 1971, plus natural increases, has been estimated at between 60,000 and 100,000. It should be emphasized that these are only estimates . . . there are no fully reliable figures available.[38]

In Ontario and Quebec, and probably elsewhere, the Black metropolitan communities are scarcely homogeneous. Studies have differentiated Blacks in the Toronto area, for example, into old-line native "Negro" Canadians, immigrants from America, West Indian immigrants, and "Negroes" who migrated from Nova Scotia.[39] A study of Blacks in Montreal used a different approach. Those living in the slum area were classified as a "core category." Those who had managed to up-grade their economic status and move into better housing were placed in a "dispersed category." West Indian immigrants were found living in both the core and dispersed areas. In addition, there existed a so-called "passing" group of light-skinned Blacks sprinkled throughout the city, students from Africa attending schools in the city, and American Blacks working, often temporarily, as entertainers, athletes, and professionals in medicine or law, the latter usually living apart from the rest of the Black community.[40]

Montreal and Toronto do not have well-defined ghettos. Instead, most Blacks there live in clusters near or within other immigrant neighbourhoods. In Nova Scotia, by contrast, even the urban Blacks are generally found only in segregated areas. Africville, crowded up against the Halifax city rubbish dump, was perhaps one of the worst slums in all Canada. After considerable delay, Africville was levelled in 1967 and a redevelopment project known as Uniak was built to replace it. Because the replacement housing was constructed in the same area, the Black community was spared the dislocation and alienation that occur when redevelopment projects forcibly uproot people and shunt them into neighbourhoods where they meet resentment and hostility.

At one time Blacks—along with native Indians, Chinese, and Japanese—were victims of so-called restrictive covenants, devices which prevented the sale of houses and land to non-Caucasians. Restrictive covenants are now illegal on the basis of court decisions in Ontario and legislation in Manitoba. Federal law has also struck a blow at discrimination in housing. Amendments to the National Housing Loan Regulations under the National Housing Act now prohibit discrimination based on race, colour, religion, or national origin for property covered by loans insured by the Central Mortgage and Housing Corporation. Most provinces now have Fair Accommodations Practices Acts, prohibiting discrimination in multiple-dwelling units, as well as Fair Housing legislation. A major problem with legislation of this type is the weakness, or absence, of enforcement machinery. In addition, the legislation often applies to housing and accommodations which the average Black cannot afford anyway.

Public Accommodations

Discrimination in this area has a hundred faces, from the subtle to the blatant. Down through the years barbers have refused to cut a Black's hair, landlords refused to rent to a Black family. Taverns in Saskatchewan and British Columbia insisted that Black patrons sit in a corner reserved for them. In 1941, only one hotel in Montreal could be depended upon not to turn Blacks away.

In July 1923, a Black watchmaker from Kitchener was refused service in a restaurant while visiting London, Ontario and took the matter to court. His suit *(Franklin v. Evans)* was dismissed the following year because the court held that the restaurant had no monopoly on service— the plaintiff was free to seek a meal elsewhere. Freedom of commerce was also given a higher priority by the courts than human rights in *Christie and Another v. York Corporation.* The court ruled that in the absence of any specific law, a merchant was free to carry on his business as he thought best, even if that meant not serving Blacks.

Restricted seating arrangements in theatres also elicited a number of court cases. In *Loew's Montreal Theatres Ltd., v. Reynolds,* the court in 1921 awarded the plaintiff fifty dollars because of a breach of contract that involved purchasing tickets for a concert. A similar decision was reached in Toronto soon after when a light-skinned woman purchased a ticket for her son at a skating rink. The boy, whose skin was much darker than his mother's, was refused admission. The court accepted the company's offer to refund twenty-five cents, the price of the ticket, to the mother. No award was made for the damages suffered through discrimination.

Segregation in the military has declined as the century has progressed. During World War I, many Blacks volunteered for military service. Only a few were permitted to enlist in local regiments, but at the same time there was strong resistance to forming all-Black units. The Minister of Militia and Defence, Colonel Sam Hughes, stated, "I will not . . . lend myself to the fad of giving [Blacks] a regiment to themselves any more than I intend to have a regiment of one-eyed men or men with yellow moustaches or red hair."[41] In fact, only one major all-Black unit was formed, a construction battalion which served in France. Meanwhile, on the home front Blacks organized their own private patriotic clubs to help raise money for the war effort.

The situation during World War II differed considerably. At first, the Canadian Army rejected Black volunteers. But in 1941 American Black volunteers were admitted, and as the war continued Blacks were accepted as equals into both the regular army and the officer corps. National headlines recorded the enlistment in the RCAF of five Black brothers from Saint John. After the war, however, evidence of segregation among returning veterans surfaced again. In particular, the Canadian Legion established Coloured War Veterans branches in both Montreal and Halifax.

Some Comparisons with the United States

For years Canadians have assumed an air of moral superiority toward the United States on the Black question. They readily observe and condemn American discriminatory practices, while remaining largely ignorant of the Black past in their own country. Yet the truth is that the political strategies of Blacks in Canada have persistently lagged at least a generation behind those adopted by Blacks in the United States. Canadian Blacks continued to subscribe to the non-militant, separate state-within-a-state precepts of Booker T. Washington—which emphasized a work ethic and vocational training that would enable Blacks to be economically independent—long after Blacks in the northern United States had discarded his central ideas. So too it is only recently that Canadian Blacks have begun to embrace the principles of the Niagara Movement, despite the fact that the meeting at which W. E. B. Du Bois, a Black leader, inaugurated the program was held at Fort Erie, Ontario in 1905. Du Bois opposed Booker T. Washington's position. He argued for integration and for Black militancy in order to secure equality of opportunity with the rest of society.

In contrast to the American experience, there have been no major civil rights confrontations in Canada involving Blacks. Instead, Canadian Blacks have traditionally relied on time and goodwill to eliminate the barriers that have obstructed their progress to equality. During the 1950s, American Blacks seized the initiative and pressed for integration of schools and public accommodations. At about the same time, new stirrings of racial pride moved these Americans to change their racial designation from "Negro" or "coloured" to "Black." By contrast, until the late 1960s the majority of Blacks in Canada apparently still wished to be called "coloured."[42] More recently, changes in attitude seem to be permeating Blacks within Nova Scotia and other provinces. One indicator is the formation of the Black United Front. Another is the implication in the remark of a Black Haligonian: "A few years ago if you called a coloured person 'Black' he would almost kill you. Now they want to be called Black,"[43] Nevertheless, uncompromising militancy remains a tactic Canadian Blacks have not tested.

Another factor that has impeded Blacks' efforts to achieve equality has been their unwillingness to participate in a single unified structure. Over the years, each wave of Blacks entering Canada has sought to retain its unique identity. This behaviour was appropriate to the Canadian "mosaic" (as opposed to the American "melting pot"), but it also markedly reduced potential Black political influence. Even now, the failure of West Indian immigrants to move into the Black mainstream has seriously impeded the Black cause. For West Indians have, or soon obtain, education and skills that could otherwise be used to benefit the entire Black community.

Clearly, Blacks in Canada, like those in the United States, want to remain in their own country. Most "Back-to-Africa" campaigns, like the Garveyite Movement, have failed. (Marcus Garvey, an explosive and charismatic man of Maroon extraction, began his Universal Negro Improvement Association in Jamaica in 1914. A branch opened in Montreal in 1919, but the movement never met with much success in Canada. In fact it created just one more division in an already divided minority.)

As noted earlier, improvements in educational attainment are helping to elevate the social and economic conditions of Blacks. The process, however, is painfully slow and likelier to benefit future than present generations. A more immediately effective approach may involve using the potentialities of mass media. American Blacks have, for example, successfully used their ample ethnic press to promote their goals. Throughout Canada's entire history, by contrast, there have been only twenty-three Black publications, with just three surviving into the 1970s. The average life of these papers has been less than two and a half years.[44] (This record contrasts with the rest of the Canadian ethnic press, which in 1970 included some two hundred publications, one with a continuous life of eighty years. Thirty-five exist in the Ukrainian language alone.) All three current Black newspapers are printed in Toronto: they are *Contrast, The Islander,* and *Africa Speaks.* Their ultimate success will depend upon the extent to which they are able to engage the widespread and long-term support of Canada's Black population.

NOTES

[1] Besides 34,445 "Negroes," the 1971 Census lists 28,025 "West Indians," many of whom would also be Black. We have simply aggregated these two numbers. For the higher "guesstimates" see Clairmont, D. H., and F. C. Wien, "Race Relations in Canada," *Sociological Focus,* 9:9, April 1976, p. 191. See also *Census of Canada, 1971,* Statistics Canada, Vol. I, Part 3, (Ottawa: Information Canada, 1972).

[2] Clairmont, Donald H., and Dennis W. Magill, *Nova Scotian Blacks: An Historical and Structural Overview* (Halifax, Institute of Public Affairs, Dalhousie University, 1970), p. 6.

[3] Walker, James W. St. G., *The Black Loyalists* (New York: Holmes & Meier, 1976), p. 7.

[4] Winks, Robin W., *The Blacks in Canada, A History* (Montreal: McGill-Queen's University Press, 1971), p. 36.

[5] Rawlyk, George A., "The Guysborough Negroes: A Study in Isolation," *Dalhousie Review,* Spring 1968, p. 26.

[6] Walker, *op. cit.,* p. 56.

[7] Landon, Fred, "The Anti-Slavery Society of Canada", *Ontario History,* 48:3, Summer 1956, p. 126.

[8] Howay, F. W., "The Negro Immigration into Vancouver Island in 1858," Royal Society of Canada, *Transactions,* 1935, sec. 2, pp. 145-56.

[9] Winks, *op. cit.,* p. 310.

[10] *Canada Gazette,* S.O.R., 1954, sec. 61, p. 1351.

[11] *House of Commons Debates,* Session 1952-53, Vol. IV, p. 4351.

[12] Winks, *op. cit.*, p. 422. The word "climate" has been removed from more recent immigration regulations. However, under the point assessment system in effect since 1967, emphasis on education and skills still militates against immigrants from non-white countries outside the Commonwealth.

[13] *Ibid.*, p. 311.

[14] Turrittin, Jane Sawyer, "Networks and Mobility: The Case of West Indian Domestics from Montserrat," *Canadian Review of Sociology and Anthropology*, 13:3, August, 1976, p. 308.

[15] Winks, *op. cit.*, p. 3.

[16] *Statutes of Upper Canada, 1793*, c. 8. Also, *33 Geo. III*, c. 7 (U.C.).

[17] Riddell, William R., "The Slave in Canada," *Journal of Negro History*, 5:3, July 1920, p. 324.

[18] Winks, Robin W., "Negro School Segregation in Ontario and Nova Scotia," *Canadian Historical Review*, 50, June 1969, pp. 164-191.

[19] *Statutes of Canada, 1849*, c. 83, s. 69.

[20] *Consolidated Statutes of Upper Canada, 1859*, c. 65, s. 1.

[21] Fergusson, C. B., *A Documentary Study of the Establishment of the Negroes in Nova Scotia* (Halifax: Public Archives of Nova Scotia, 1948), p. 169.

[22] Cited in Winks, *op. cit.*, p. 167.

[23] Cited in *ibid.*, p. 169.

[24] *Ibid.*, p. 170.

[25] Clairmont, D. H., *et al.*, *A Socio-Economic Study and Recommendations; Sunnyville, Lincolnville and Upper Big Tracadie, Guysborough County, Nova Scotia* (Halifax: Institute of Public Affairs, Dalhousie University, 1965), chapter 4.

[26] *Simmons v. Chatham* (1861), 21 U.C.Q.B., 75; and *Dunn v. Windsor* (1884), 6 O.R., 125.

[27] *Washington v. Trustees of Charlotteville*, (1854), 11 U.C.Q.B., 569.

[28] Winks, *op. cit.*, p. 191.

[29] Head, Wilson A., *The Black Presence in the Canadian Mosaic* (Toronto: Ontario Human Rights Commission, 1975), p. 89.

[30] *Ibid.*, p. 60.

[31] *Ibid.*, p. 71.

[32] Potter, Harold H., "Negroes in Canada," *Race*, 3:1, November 1961, p. 49.

[33] Turrittin, *op. cit.*, p. 314. Financial and vocational training courses are available through the Manpower Training Program, but information on these resources is often unknown to the immigrants.

[34] Head, *op. cit.*, p. 86.

[35] Ramcharan, Subhas, "The Economic Adaptation of West Indians in Toronto, Canada", *Canadian Review of Sociology and Anthropoligy*, 13:3, August 1976, p. 299.

[36] *Ibid.*, p. 301.

[37] Head, *op. cit.*, p. 221.

[38] *Ibid.*, p. 21.

[39] Hill, Daniel G., Jr., *Negroes in Toronto: A Sociological Study of a Minority Group*, unpublished Ph.D. thesis, University of Toronto, 1960.

[40] Potter, *op. cit.*, pp. 40-1.

[41] Cited in Winks, *The Blacks in Canada*, p. 314.

[42] Winks, Robin W., "The Canadian Negro: The Problem of Identity," in Elliot, Jean L. *Minority Canadians 2, Immigrant Groups* (Scarborough: Prentice-Hall, 1971), p. 96.

[43] See Clairmont and Magill, *Nova Scotian Blacks*, p. 8.

[44] Winks, *The Blacks in Canada*, *op. cit.*, p. 391.

Chapter 5

CHINESE AND JAPANESE

In the past, Chinese and Japanese were collectively referred to in Canada as "Orientals." For the better part of a century, in fact, Canadians worried about a growing "Oriental problem"—or, as it was often termed, "the yellow peril," a phrase coined by Kaiser Wilhelm of Germany in 1895 to describe the growing international power of Japan.[1] Nowadays, in line with the increased appreciation of minority contributions to the nation's life, the word "Oriental" is generally avoided, since it seems to connote scorn and disrespect. Except where the label is historically appropriate, we shall also avoid using it. Instead, our attention will be directed to the 118,815 Chinese and the 37,260 Japanese who were Canadian residents in 1971, and to their predecessors in this country.[2]

We begin by reviewing the periods of immigration and of exclusion experienced by the Chinese and Japanese. We also examine in some detail the World War II evacuation of Japanese from the West Coast, since this episode marked the nadir of official Canadian policy toward a nonwhite minority. Discussion of specific problems faced by Chinese and Japanese, such as denial of the vote, restrictions on employment, and (to a lesser extent) limitations on schooling and housing, are preceded by a more general consideration of the racial prejudices they encountered. Finally, attention is paid to the changes and advances registered by the Japanese and, to a lesser degree, by the Chinese since the mid-1940s.

Immigration and Exclusion

During the 1850s, the Fraser River gold rush brought the first wave of Chinese immigrants to Canada. Initially they came from California, where they had worked as labourers and miners in the Gold Rush of 1849. Later immigrants came directly from China. When a given mine was exhausted a few Chinese returned home, but most remained in British Columbia, transferring to occupations like general labour, domestic service, gardening, and laundry work.

A second major group of Chinese immigrants came with the building of the Canadian Pacific Railroad in the 1880s. British Columbia had pressured the federal government for a railroad that would link it to eastern Canada; to raise the necessary labour force the federal authorities permitted the Onderdonk Construction Company to import about seventeen thousand Chinese labourers from the Kwantung province of

China.[3] Only male Chinese were allowed to enter. The idea was that they would provide cheap labour during the construction of the railroad and then return immediately to China. The exclusion of Chinese women, and the severe social sanctions imposed for relationships with white women, accentuated the intended transitory nature of the Chinese work force.

When the Canadian Pacific Railroad was completed in November 1885, many Chinese had not accumulated the fortune they had expected. Yet neither the railroad nor the federal government was willing to pay their return fare to China. The Six Companies of San Francisco, which were benevolent societies caring for the welfare of Chinese immigrants from the six districts of Kwantung province, did hire four steamers to transport those wishing to go back. A reduced fare of twenty-five dollars per head was generally available, while for those sixty years or over there would be free passage and a present of fifteen dollars.[4] It is not known how many took advantage of this offer, but apparently most of the Chinese remained in Port Hammond, Yale, and Victoria, and in the coastal area around Vancouver. Often they were completely destitute. Their choice was to beg, steal, or starve.

Since economic conditions were unstable, these men became a large reservoir of cheap labour, in potential or actual competition with whites. They were good workers and in order to survive they were willing to take jobs at almost any wage. Both facts generated bitter resentment among white organized labour, which saw the Chinese as enemies, snatching away employment and undercutting wage agreements. Compounding the problem was a small but steady flow of new Chinese immigrants who were responding to rumours of jobs available in the western provinces.

In 1878, the Workingman's Protective Association was formed in Victoria to "protect" white labourers. Other anti-Chinese groups soon followed: for example, the Knights of Labour in 1884. The Nanaimo Trades Organization, a more moderate anti-Chinese group, was organized in 1885. These labour organizations later helped form or supported groups like the Anti-Mongolian League and the Asiatic Exclusion League.

Labour was aided in these endeavours by groups such as the Liberal League and the Blue Ribbon Clubs of Victoria, public-spirited citizens concerned about the "morals" of the Chinese. Some of the charges stemmed from the existence of secret Chinese societies like the Chinese Freemasons (founded in 1862), the Chinese Benevolent Society, and the Chinese Empire Reform Association. In fact, such associations had long been a legitimate part of local social order in the Kwantung province of China.[5] Other concerns involved Chinese use of opium. From time to time the substance was prohibited or, as in Victoria, a five-hundred-dollar den licence was required.[6] Ironically, though, while British Columbia was banning the drug, the federal government considered opium a common article of trade, not unlike the British who shipped opium from India to China in the nineteenth century and fought the Opium Wars of 1839 to protect their commercial interests.

Other forms of harrassment were also common. For example, in 1876 a bill was introduced in the British Columbia legislature imposing an annual ten-dollar tax on every Chinese male aged eighteen and above who wore long hair in the shape of a tail or queue. Two years later, it was recommended that no males with hair longer than five-and-one-half inches be employed by the Canadian Pacific Railroad. The rationale for such legislation involved health standards. The real intent, of course, was for the province to tax or restrain aliens without appearing to do just that, since such action was exclusively within the jurisdiction of the federal government.

In response to this provincial hostility, the federal government on July 5, 1884, established the Royal Commission on Chinese Immigration. Members of the Commission visited Chinatowns in San Francisco and in British Columbia. The Commission Report noted that the great majority of British Columbia's citizens were anti-Chinese and eager for some form of restrictive legislation. This was true despite the fact that the material (economic) advantages of Chinese immigration were considerable. Coal mining, fish canning, and market gardening, the Report indicated, could not have progressed so well without Chinese labour, nor would the Canadian Pacific Railroad have been constructed within a reasonable length of time. The commissioners also pointed out that white labourers, as soon as they became contractors, were the first to employ Chinese. [7]

As resentment toward the Chinese grew, changes were sought in the immigration rules. Most pressures for such legal restrictions came of course from British Columbia. As early as 1872, requests were sent from the provincial legislature to the federal government, asking for the imposition of a head tax on all Chinese entering the province. The request failed. In 1875, the city of Victoria passed a motion barring Chinese from employment on public works in that city. In 1878, a licence fee of thirty dollars was imposed on all Chinese working in Victoria. This in turn led to a general strike of Chinese in that city.

Premier Walkem of British Columbia attempted to get an anti-Chinese clause inserted in Canadian Pacific Railroad contracts. The attempt was unsuccessful, and construction of the railroad began in 1880 with both white and Chinese labourers. In 1884, the provincial legislature passed a Chinese Immigration Act making it unlawful for Chinese to enter British Columbia, and a Chinese Regulation Act prohibiting the use of opium, specifying the size of dwelling rooms occupied by Chinese, and requiring the purchase of a one hundred dollar licence by every Chinese over the age of fourteen years. Both of these Acts were later disallowed by the federal government.

The first federal head tax on incoming Chinese commenced in 1885. The rate was fifty dollars. This was increased to one hundred dollars effective in 1901, and to five hundred dollars in 1904. The tax was paid by Chinese immigrants as a condition of entry, though exemptions were made for consular officers, clergymen, tourists, merchants, and students. As a money-making device, this impost was fairly successful. Between 1886 and 1923, Chinese paid more than twenty-two million dollars in head taxes, with half that sum reverting to the province of British Columbia.[8] As a means of stemming the flow of immigrants, the levy was a comparative failure. Some Chinese were smuggled into the country inside the huge coal bunkers of the Oriental steamships; others arrived as tourists and simply melted into the population of a Chinatown; still others resorted to the expediency of paying one hundred dollars to join a business firm in China, thus becoming bona fide merchants not subject to the tax.[9] The upshot was that the Chinese soon became solidly entrenched in farming, service occupations, and small businesses.

Additional measures restricting Chinese entry even more were passed during the first half of the present century. For example, a 1903 Parliamentary enactment required every Asian immigrant not covered by a special statute or treaty to possess two hundred dollars upon landing in Canada.[10] For determined immigrants, though, there were always ways around such impediments. If they lacked the necessary savings, perhaps they could borrow from fellow countrymen already living in Canada and then repay that amount (plus interest) in the years after their arrival. All this requirement really did was to increase the economic hardship of new immigrants rather than dissuade them from coming.

Gradually, it became clear to legislators that the only sure way to stop the Chinese was to forbid their entry entirely. This approach was enshrined in the Chinese Immigration Act of 1923, more commonly known as the Chinese Exclusion Act. Its effectiveness is apparent when one considers that between 1923 and 1947, when the Act was repealed, only forty-four Chinese immigrants entered the country legally.[11]

Quite early on, some Chinese began drifting eastward to set down roots at various railroad towns. By 1890, they were operating hand laundries and restaurants in Calgary. There they shared a quiet life of their own, pursuing daily activities within the framework of the more general social environment. "They were not liked but they were needed, and as such they were confined to their position within the larger community."[12]

Prejudice, discrimination, and scapegoating dogged the Chinese. For example, when Calgary experienced an outbreak of smallpox in 1892 and three of nine persons who contacted the disease died, the Chinese were blamed as carriers from British Columbia. Public attacks increased until it became necessary to call in the mounted police to prevent possible lynchings.

Similarly, when the Chinese wished to expand their district in Calgary (and elsewhere), they were encumbered by a host of problems, including the refusal of many people to sell them additional land or dwellings. Attempts at boycotting were instituted in order to force the Chinese out of business. In 1913, it was proposed that all Chinese in Calgary be photographed and fingerprinted for identification purposes.[13] All this activity, it should be noted, was directed toward a mere 485 Chinese, compared with 43,704 whites who lived in Calgary as of 1911.[14]

Until recently, however, despite a scattering of Chinese and Japanese in more easterly provinces, the "Oriental problem" was primarily of concern to British Columbia. There some fifty thousand Chinese and Japanese resided, while only twenty thousand were spread throughout the rest of the country. In British Columbia there was one Chinese or Japanese person for thirteen whites, a much higher ratio than anywhere else in Canada.

Japanese immigration posed less of a problem, in part because the numbers involved were smaller, and in part because Canada and Japan eventually reached a "gentlemen's agreement" on the subject. The first Japanese immigrant to Canada was a nineteen-year-old sailor who remained ashore in 1877 when his ship returned to the Orient.[15] Occasionally, Japanese shipwrecked at sea also managed to drift to the west coast of Canada. But not until 1885 did immigration to Canada begin in earnest. Even then, many of the Japanese entering Canadian ports were transients who either stayed for a season and returned home or travelled to the United States. Indeed, the census of 1901 showed only 4,738 Japanese living in Canada.

Most of the early immigrants were poverty-stricken farmers and fishermen, seeking the economic opportunity that they could not find at home. One group, the Okinawans, were looked upon as socially and intellectually inferior country cousins. The Okinawans living in Alberta remained isolated from the major Japanese communities and the coastal settlements of British Columbia. They were also spared the fate that befell the West Coast Japanese during World War II.

Until the outbreak of World War II, most Japanese remained clustered near their ports of entry in British Columbia and lived in communities with their fellow countrymen. The province provided work in three major industries: fishing, coal mining, and lumbering. The climate, the coastline, the mountains, and all the natural beauty of the province served to remind the Japanese of their homeland.

Canadian Chinese made no attempts to pool their resources with Canadian Japanese in order to combat their common grievances more effectively. The Chinese seemed indifferent to political and economic discrimination, while the Japanese resented and opposed it. Similarly, the paternalistic attitude of the Japanese government toward its nationals residing in Canada and the supportive role of Japanese consular officials were in startling contrast to the condition of the Chinese, who had no one in authority to support them.

In addition, Japanese felt themselves superior to Chinese and, conversely, Chinese resented being displaced by Japanese in those industries which they had been first to enter. In periods of high unemployment, employers would even pit the two nationalities against each other to see which would accept the smaller wage. Adding to the estrangement was Japan's continued aggression against China in the Far East, beginning with the Sino-Japanese War of 1894 and terminating only with Japan's defeat in World War II. The peak of Chinese opposition occurred in 1937 when Japan's armies were ravaging the coastal provinces of China. Chinese grocers refused to handle vegetables grown by Japanese farmers in the Fraser Valley of British Columbia. Chinese consumers also boycotted Japanese merchants.

While provincial legislation could not directly deal with aliens, since they were foreign nationals and thus a federal responsibility, there was always the hope that subtle legal distinctions between nationalities and races might somehow succeed. This helps explain the British Columbia law, first passed in 1900, which required every immigrant in the province, when so ordered, to write an application to the provincial secretary in some European language. Failure or inability to comply could result in a five-hundred-dollar fine, a year's imprisonment, or deportation. When the Japanese ambassador protested, the federal government disallowed the legislation. Undaunted, British Columbia enacted similar laws in 1902, 1903, 1905, 1907, and 1908. All were disallowed by the federal government.

United States prohibitions on further Japanese immigration in 1907 led to fears that Canada might be flooded with them, and induced the federal government to work out a plan or informal agreement with Japan that restricted the immigration rate to four hundred workers annually, plus wives and children. An amendment to this "gentlemen's agreement" in June 1928 set the annual quota at one hundred and fifty immigrants including wives and children. The "picture bride" system was also terminated in 1928. It has been established in 1908 to promote Japanese "family building." The plan involved exchanging photographs once relatives of the immigrant found a woman in Japan whom they regarded as suitable. If the would-be groom liked the picture, the "marriage" would be registered in Japan. The bride would then come to Canada after the groom had arranged for a passport.[16]

Most first-generation Japanese-Canadians (the *Issei*), were traditionally oriented, familial, unskilled workers, non-English speakers, and strong believers in a close-knit, hierarchical community structure. As time went on, they concentrated overwhelmingly within Vancouver itself. By 1920, about nineteen thousand out of twenty-two thousand lived in that city, mainly within "Little Tokyos." Group relationships had a strong influence on the Issei. The family system was the key element in the internal solidarity of the community. Important linkages were provided by a vast complex of associations and clubs, involving some 230 secular and religious associations in British Columbia, of which 84 were in Vancouver alone.[17]

The second generation Japanese (the *Nisei*) had more education, spoke English, exhibited greater occupational mobility, but also were often, as were many other second-generation Canadians, torn between the old and new ways. Both Issei and Nisei stand in some contrast to the *Sansei*, a term that refers both to the third generation and to the Japanese immigrants of more recent years.

Evacuation of the Japanese

Before World War II, the Chinese generally experienced more discrimination than the Japanese. The latter were well organized, with associations able to speak for the entire community. Japanese could also rely on the government of Japan for a certain amount of support. Japan was an ally of Britain, and the array of commercial and navigational treaties between the Empire and Japan proved a bulwark against discriminatory statutes passed by the British Columbia legislature. The Japanese government was often successful in protesting these statutes through its ambassador in Ottawa.

The situation of the Chinese was rather different. The government of China was weak and internally torn. Diplomatically, not even consular representation existed between China and Canada until 1909. Domestically, the Chinese lacked leadership and organization. Some associations could be found in various Chinatowns, but they were ineffective in protecting the rights of Chinese. Even the large Chinese Benevolent Association, founded at Vancouver in 1884, functioned primarily as a mutual aid society for the benefit of the aged and the impoverished. It never wielded any political influence. With no united front in Canada, and no backing from their home government, Chinese in Canada were an easy mark for discrimination.

During World War I, both China and Japan were on the side of the allies and declared war against Germany. During the early stages of the war, many Chinese aliens returned to China because of the growing unemployment in British Columbia. China furnished thousands of labourers to work behind the lines in France, and many of these people passed through Canada under guard on the way to Europe. Some Chinese Canadians served in the Canadian armed forces.

The Canadian Japanese Association sought permission for Japanese to enlist in the Canadian army and navy. (In 1900, Japanese had offered to raise and equip their own unit to fight in the Boer War, but their offer was rejected.) A "Japanese Volunteer Corps" of 202 men began training in Vancouver in early 1916. Since there were insufficient numbers to form a separate battalion of 1,100 men, however, the group was disbanded.[18] While no official statements were ever issued, there is little doubt that the government's reluctance to encourage the enlistment of Chinese and Japanese stemmed from the assumption that this would be a prelude to the demand for voting rights. Nevertheless, 196 Japanese volunteers were accepted into the Canadian army during World War I, and 53 died in military service.

During World War II, the relative positions of Chinese and Japanese in the Canadian social hierarchy were reversed. Now, the Japanese were to experience far more drastic discrimination and persecution than the Chinese ever suffered. To be sure, with the entry of Canada into the European war, the Japanese Canadian Citizens League had pledged "deepest loyalty and devotion" to Canada by offering the services of Japanese for the war effort. As of the summer of 1941, Japanese communities had subscribed $340,200 to the Victory Loan Drive.[19] But while the federal government accepted these offers of help, it decided that citizens of Chinese and Japanese ancestry would be exempted from conscription for military service. And meanwhile, a more diffuse anti-Japanese sentiment was continuing to mount.

As early as Halloween night of 1939, shortly after Canada had entered the war against Germany, a mob of three hundred whites smashed plate glass windows and looted stores in the Japanese sector of Vancouver. Fearing the danger of subversive activities in the event of war with Japan, the federal government later ordered the compulsory registration of all Japanese. The task of registration was begun by the RCMP on March 4, 1941 and completed in late August. Each person was required to carry a registration card at all times. White cards were issued to persons born in Canada, pink cards to naturalized citizens, and yellow cards to alien Japanese. All firearms and explosives in the possession of Japanese were confiscated by the government, supposedly to forestall open conflict between Chinese and Japanese.

Events precipitating the evacuation of the Japanese from British Columbia included the December 7, 1941 attack on Pearl Harbor by the Japanese air force and navy, and the Japanese military strike against Hong Kong the next day. The garrison at Hong Kong capitulated on Christmas Day 1941, and the two-thousand-man Canadian contingent stationed there was killed or captured. Widespread fear of an imminent Japanese invasion of the West Coast quickly arose. Immediate action by the federal government included a declaration of war against Japan, the arresting of 38 Japanese allegedly dangerous to national security, the impounding of 1,200 fishing boats owned or operated by Nisei or naturalized citizens, and the closing of 59 Japanese-language schools and three vernacular newspapers published in Vancouver. A second, special registration of all Japanese was mandated on December 16, 1941. No differentiation was made this time on the basis of citizenship. Public agitation and emotionalism against the Japanese reached a fever pitch by mid-December when hundreds of Japanese were discharged from their jobs on railroads, factories, and mills, creating a spectre of heavy unemployment.

An Order-in-Council (P.C. 365) was issued on January 16, 1942 authorizing the evacuation of Japanese nationals from the West Coast. This Order was amended on the 24th of February to include all persons of the Japanese race. Implementation regulations were issued on February 26th. A "Defence Zone" one hundred miles in width was created; all persons within it of Japanese origin—whether Canadian-born, naturalized Canadian citizens, or aliens—were forcibly removed from their homes and places of business. According to the 1941 census, there were 23,149 persons of Japanese ancestry in Canada, representing less than one-fifth of one percent of the total Canadian population, Some 22,096 of them lived in British Columbia; however, the majority were living in the coastal region and by October 1942, 20,881 persons had been uprooted and evacuated from their homes.[20] Japanese living east of the Cascades and in other provinces of Canada were not evacuated. The evacuation program extended over a nine-month period and cost the government fifteen million dollars.[21]

There was a precedent for the evacuation program. In 1915, about six thousand persons of German descent had been placed in internment camps across Canada. With the outbreak of World War II in Europe, German and Italian aliens living in Canada were also required to register and report regularly with the Registrar of Enemy Aliens. Moreover, under the provisions of the War Measures Act, the federal government could restrict, control, evacuate, and even deport Japanese without bringing charges against them. The Cabinet was the sole judge of the necessity of the measures to be taken, and was not subject to review by any court.

Most Japanese did not resist evacuation. Their cooperation reflected their cultural norms of duty and obligation, conformity and obedience. The entire evacuation program itself, however, was characterized by complete disregard of the legal and constitutional guarantees for the protection of liberty and property. Property was confiscated and quickly disposed of without consent of the owners; persons were arrested by police without arrest warrants; homes and places of business were searched by police without warrants.

During the early stages of the evacuation, conditions were chaotic. People had to move on less than twenty-four hours' notice and were given no time to make arrangements for the care of property or household goods. Automobiles, trucks, radios, and cameras were impounded, and sold at public auction a few months later. The only Japanese permitted to remain in the coastal area were a few institutionalized mental cases, ninety-four persons who were partners in mixed marriages, and about a hundred children who were their offspring. As Adachi remarks, "Intermarriage, then, was the magic elixir that converted security risks into bona fide Canadians."[22]

Evacuees were relocated in areas east of the Cascades and in the prairie provinces. Internment camps were provided, whose conditions left much to be desired. Some men were put to work in the sugar beet fields of Alberta, where there was a serious labour shortage. Others toiled on road-building projects. The men earned $50 gross per month, with $22.50 deducted for room and board and $20.00 for support of their families, leaving a net of $7.50 per month for all other expenses.[23]

Control over property, principally in British Columbia, owned by the evacuees was vested in the Custodian of Enemy Alien Property, who exercised wide discretionary powers of management or disposal. Homes, lands, businesses, and equipment were frequently sold over the protests of their owners at remarkably low prices.[24] Fishing boats and gear, for example, were seized immediately after the attack on Pearl Harbor, and were later sold to white fishermen who had been competitors of the Japanese. Given both the war hysteria and the long smouldering resentment against the Japanese, it is clear that:

> . . . the arbitrary sale of their property by the Custodian bore no relationship to the security, defence, peace, order or welfare of Canada; unless, however, the order or welfare of Canada required that their property be sold so that their roots in the West Coast be severed, and that they would be discouraged from returning.[25]

As noted above, legal justification for the repressive actions against Canada's Japanese population lay in the War Measures Act, a statute that affected other groups during the war as well. For example, the Communist Party and all fascist organizations were banned. The Jehovah's Witnesses were declared illegal, allegedly because their pacifist orientation would somehow reduce efficient prosecution of the war. The RCMP was the primary administrative vehicle for these and other restrictive actions. Besides being in charge of the evacuation and subsequent internment of the Japanese, it placed restraints on the leadership and associational integrity of Italians and Ukrainians.[26]

The treatment accorded Japanese under the War Measures Act was, however, far worse that that directed to the others. The explanation almost certainly lies in racial animosity. Japan, to be sure, was an Axis power (that is, Germany, Japan, and Italy), but Canada's major enemy was Germany. Nearly all the Canadian military forces were operating in the European theatre. Japan never attempted an invasion of British Columbia, but German submarines operated within Canadian Arctic waters. A few American freighters were shelled by Japanese submarines off the California coast, but these attacks were puny in comparison to the Nazi submarine campaigns in the Atlantic. Yet there was no hysteria over a possible invasion of the Atlantic coastal area by Germany. And even though German and Italian aliens were required to register, it was not suggested that Germans living in Canada be evacuated and interned. Indeed, except for Hutterites living on the prairies, Germans living in Canada were little restricted.[27]

By contrast, sensational rumours of Japanese aiding and abetting the enemy and false stories of sabotage at Pearl Harbor were repeated as matters of fact in Canada. Yet one of the major ironies of the war was that persons of Japanese descent in Hawaii were never subjected to evacuation or internment. And this is true despite the fact that there were some 160,000 persons of Japanese ancestry in Hawaii who constituted 38 percent of the Hawaiian population, while the Japanese in British Columbia accounted for only 2.7 percent of its total population.

Canadians cannot claim that in their repression of Japanese residents they were following the American lead. On the contrary, British Columbia was already cleared of Japanese well before a similar evacuation was begun from the west coast of the United States. Canada's evacuation order, in fact, was issued more than a month before the equivalent American order, as Forrest LaViolette notes.

> Canadians are disposed to believe that American sentiment was a determining factor in making necessary the decision for complete evacuation in Canada. But the San Diego Union on January 22 and 29, and again on March 3, 1942, held up the Canadian decision and plan as the one which the United States should follow.[28]

While all the arguments and justification for the evacuation were based on the issue of national security, the ultimate cause seems to have been a composite of racial animosity, economic and political aggrandizement, and an accumulation of years of misinformation, half-truths, unfounded fears, and insinuations about people from the Orient. In due course, the evacuation of the Japanese became an end in itself. Once the Japanese had been removed from the coastal areas, British Columbia began efforts to exclude them permanently. This sort of motive, rather than "national security," explains the speedy and arbitrary disposal of Japanese property.

Virulent official anti-Japanese sentiment also lasted longer in Canada than in America. In particular, three Orders-in-Council (P.C. 7355, 7356, and 7357) were issued on December 15, 1945 under the authority of the War Measures Act for deporting to Japan persons of Japanese ancestry. The Minister of Labour could thereby require deportation of Japanese nationals, naturalized or Canadian-born Japanese, and the wives and children of any of the above. These orders were not revoked until 1947.

Meanwhile, some ten thousand allegedly voluntary requests for deportation were received by the government. In due course, 3,964 Japanese were "voluntarily repatriated" to war-torn Japan. The degree of voluntarism is open to serious question. It has been alleged, in fact, that natural-born and naturalized Japanese Canadians were encouraged by government agents to sign forms for deportation as an act of "cooperation," and that the government subsequently claimed that these signed forms were specific requests for repatriation.[29]

However this may be, it is certain that wartime security had no bearing on the deportation orders. They were issued three and a half months after Japan's surrender and its occupation by Allied forces. Nor has any evidence ever been uncovered of subversive activities by Japanese Canadians during the war itself. On the contrary, despite the discriminatory treatment received by Japanese in Canada for nearly a century, they never exhibited vindictiveness or retaliation. One can only conclude, therefore, that the orders reflected an anti-Japanese hostility based on racial differences. As Prime Minister Trudeau later remarked, forced deportation of Japanese Canadians "didn't quite happen . . . but the fact that it could have been contemplated (and legally carried out) is a frightening thing."[30] Only once before in Canada's history had there been a similar expulsion of a people; that occurred in 1755, when some three thousand Acadians were exiled to various English colonies in North America.

The evacuation and internment had a massive effect on the subsequent social geography of Canadian Japanese. Initially, though, the placing of evacuees in rural and urban areas of central and eastern Canada only served to spread the feelings of antagonism toward the Japanese. For example, despite critical labour shortages on Alberta's beet farms, the Albertans resented the influx of Japanese. Cities could not be visited by Japanese who were housed in camps or on nearby farms. The city council in Lethbridge, Alberta specifically banned Japanese girls who had worked as domestics from carrying on that occupation within city limits. As an additional indignity, Japanese were banned from beer parlours in the province. The dispersal of Japanese throughout the other nine provinces did not solve the "Japanese problem."

Comparatively speaking, the evacuated Japanese found their best acceptance in Manitoba. Not only were they considered to be an economic asset to farmers in the beet fields, but also newspapers and public opinion were favourable to them, with the *Winnipeg Free Press* taking a particularly vigorous stand against racism. By contrast, considerable hostility to evacuees was expressed by municipal councils in eastern Canada. The city of Chatham, Ontario flatly refused to accept any Japanese. Protests were made when three Japanese families moved into Grimsby, Ontario. Toronto at first declined to admit any evacuees. And while the Board of Control later relaxed the ban, allowing some seven hundred Japanese by the end of 1943, Toronto thereafter reverted to a closed city. Moreover, on November 17, 1944 the Toronto Police Commission refused to issue the necessary occupational and premise licences to Nisei evacuees who wished to establish independent businesses.[31]

Few Japanese returned to British Columbia after the war. Vancouver lost its position as leadership centre, and the Japanese community there never regained its previous level of commercial activity. Whether British Columbia was beneficiary of the government's wartime policy, since it got what it had long wanted, or was victim, as most historians would judge Spain when its preferred policy of expelling the Moors was carried out, depends ultimately on the values one holds. In his address to the Japanese Diet in 1976, Prime Minister Trudeau was moved to express the guilt of Canadians over this ugly chapter in Canadian racial history. Those who actually formulated and carried out the wartime policies have not expressed regret or admitted error. (By contrast most officials involved in the American evacuation have acknowledged that it was completely unjustified.) Perhaps the best retrospective summation was made by Prime Minister Lester Pearson, speaking at the opening of the Japanese Canadian Cultural Centre in 1964:

> That action by the Canadian government of the day—though taken under the strains and fears and pressures and irrationalities of war— was a black mark against Canada's traditional fairness and devotion to the principles of human rights. We have no reason to be proud of this episode.[32]

Racial Prejudices

Anti-Oriental dread has historically been among the most persistent forms of racism in Canada. While considerable opposition and hostility has sometimes been aroused by the mass immigration of non-British peoples from Europe, Chinese and Japanese usually elicited an even stronger reaction. They were seen as a biologically distinct and inferior group which could never, in the nature of things, become part of Canadian society. James Shaver Woodsworth, a Methodist minister, first national leader of the Co-operative Commonwealth Federation (forerunner of the New Democratic Party), and a man of so pronounced a social conscience that he has been called the "saint" of Canadian politics, wrote in 1908 that Chinese and Japanese should be excluded without question from Canada. As he saw it, "It is true that they may be able to do much of the rough work, for which it is difficult to secure sufficient white labour; but where they enter, the whites are out, and out permanently. . . . They constitute an entirely distinct class or caste. . . . The Orientals cannot be assimilated."[33]

A similar viewpoint animated a 1921 resolution of the British Columbia legislature which called for the Immigration Act to be amended "so as nearly as possible to totally restrict the immigration of Asiatics into the province, keeping in view the wishes of the people of British Columbia that this province should be reserved for people of the European race."[34] This view was still being officially repeated a quarter of a century later. Two years after World War II ended, Prime Minister Mackenzie King stated for the record and on the floor of Parliament:

> The policy of the government is to foster the growth of the population of Canada by the encouragement of immigration. The government will seek by legislation, regulation and vigorous administration, to ensure the careful selection and permanent settlement of such numbers of immigrants as can be advantageously absorbed in our national economy.

He then added:

> It is a matter of domestic policy. . . . The people of Canada do not wish as a result of mass immigration to make a fundamental alteration in the character of our population. Large scale immigration from the Orient would change the fundamental composition of the Canadian population.[35]

Nor was the outlook of organized labour much different as recently as the immediate post-World War II years. Labour groups were given the opportunity to express themselves on the immigration issue before the Senate Committee on Immigration and Labour in 1946, 1947, and 1948. Here is what a spokesman from the Trades and Labour Congress (forerunner of the Canadian Labour Congress) had to say, albeit with some nice circumspection:

> We recognize the need for selection and the exclusion of all races that cannot properly be assimilated into the national life of Canada. . . . It must be recognized that there are citizens of other countries who may be good brothers and sisters internationally, but yet would not be good brothers and sisters-in-law to Canadians. Experience has clearly demonstrated that because of this fact, certain nationals who have in the past been admitted to Canada remain as a distinct race and will remain a problem for future generations.[36]

A similar racial prejudice almost certainly lay behind many legislative and administrative actions that at first glance might seem unobjectionable. For example, in 1890 the British Columbia legislature passed the Coal Mines Regulation Amendment Act. Ostensibly, the statute was a safety measure. Its real purpose was unveiled in a court decision which found that:

> . . . the regulations . . . were not really aimed at the regulation of coal mines at all, but were in truth devised to deprive the Chinese, naturalized or not, of the ordinary rights of the inhabitants of British Columbia and, in effect, to prohibit their continued residence in that province, since it prohibited their earning their living in that province.[37]

Nor did age, however venerable, protect against racial discrimination either. Elderly and impoverished Chinese and Japanese were denied the right to apply for admission into the British Columbia Provincial Home in 1936.[38]

Much the same reading may be given to some of the delaying tactics employed by the Department of Immigration. For instance, after the Supreme Court in the 1953 case of *R. and McDonell v. Leong Be Chai* ordered the department to accept the application by the son of a Canadian citizen of Chinese origin for admission into Canada, it took the department a year to review the request. During that time, the father died, leaving the son no Canadian citizen to sponsor him. The department then ruled that the son was inadmissible.[39]

A long miscellany of provincial legislation also testifies to the near omnipresence of racial prejudice. The problem addressed was sometimes petty in the extreme. But that pettiness itself is a symptom of something more serious and baleful that was troubling the country's collective political soul. Examples include a 1914 Ontario law that prohibited white women from working in Chinese business places,[40] and a 1915 Quebec law that increased licence and inspection fees for public laundries. In the latter instance, an exempting clause made the raises inapplicable to laundries operated by charitable organizations or corporate enterprises, so that only Chinese establishments were affected.[41]

The Franchise

A fundamental right of citizens in a democracy is to participate in the decision making of their government. One principal means is through voting in elections. Yet the Chinese and Japanese—like several other groups discussed in this volume—have experienced a long history of franchise denials.

Chinese residents of British Columbia were denied the vote as early as 1875. The prohibition was applied to other Asians in an 1895 law which covered provincial elections; in 1896 this was extended to include municipal elections.[42] Surprisingly, while Chinese were not allowed to vote, they were counted in the population figures used to determine the number of federal members of Parliament allocated to British Columbia. "This was a special concession made to the Pacific province to help lure it into Confederation; no other province was allowed to count either natives or orientals when it came to enjoying federal grants or popular representation."[43]

Barely a decade later, Saskatchewan barred its Chinese from voting. In both provinces, the denial of the vote depended on race rather than nationality. Thus, while British Columbia generally conferred voting privileges on persons of British nationality, exceptions were made for those whose ancestry was Chinese or Japanese. These voting exclusions were upheld by various lower courts; by the Privy Council, which in 1903 sustained a British Columbia law disqualifying Japanese; and by the Supreme Court, which in 1914 sustained British Columbia's denial of the franchise to the Chinese.[44]

Denial of the provincial franchise was a two-edged sword, since exclusion from the voters' lists could also adversely affect employment opportunities. For instance, under provisions of British Columbia's Liquor Licence Act of 1899, persons of Chinese and Japanese background were effectively denied licences to sell liquor.Only those whose names were on voting lists could obtain a licence. Chinese and Japanese could similarly not practise law or pharmacy, because eligibility to be a student or apprentice in these fields was limited to "those who would, if the age of twenty-one years, be entitled to be placed on the Voters' List under the Provincial Elections Act."[45]

It was only a matter of time until provincial voting restrictions against the Chinese and Japanese would be extended to the federal level. This happened in 1919, when the Members of Parliament from British Columbia objected to the fact that Chinese and Japanese could still vote in national elections. As a result, a new section was inserted in the Dominion Franchise Bill of 1920 which read:

> Persons who, by the laws of any province of Canada, are disqualified from voting (for) a member of the Legislative Assembly of such province in respect of race, shall not be qualified to vote in such province under the provisions of this act.[46]

The only exceptions involved those who had served in World War I.[47]

In the 1930s, Japan invaded China and committed acts of aggression against the Chinese people. To a degree, many Canadians felt great sympathy for China's sufferings. Yet British Columbia made no efforts either before or during World War II to extend voting rights to Canadians of Chinese origin. Only in 1947 did it remove voting restrictions against the Chinese. Two years later, it extended voting rights to its Japanese residents. All franchise restrictions on both groups have now been eliminated at both federal and provincial levels.

Employment

Chinese and Japanese entered this country at a time when their labour was urgently needed in railroad construction and in the lumber and mining industries. Most Canadians thought that the work would be temporary and, once over, the Asians would return to their homelands. When they did not return, resentment set in. For the next hundred years, Chinese and Japanese would find themselves subject to severe job discrimination.

As already noted, after they were denied the vote Chinese and Japanese were automatically excluded from all jobs requiring a licence. Moreover, since no one has a claim on a licence by right, there could be no judicial redress. British Columbia devised other discriminatory tactics to a similar end. Chinese and Japanese were legally prohibited from direct or indirect employment by any contractor holding a British Columbia Department of Public Works contract. Japanese were denied public school teaching positions. A 1925 Male Minimum Wage Act was cleverly designed to affect Chinese and Japanese adversely by setting the minimum wage above that normally paid to those groups. The intent of the law was to diminish the attractiveness of cheap labour to employers in the lumbering industry and thereby encourage greater use of white labour. A federal Department of Marine and Fisheries regulation also reduced the number of fishing licences that could be issued to "other than white British subjects and Canadian Indians."[48]

Organized labour vigorously supported job discrimination directed against the Chinese and Japanese. The reason lay in a narrowly conceived economic self-interest. Sometimes, to be sure, there was no direct competition between whites and the Chinese or Japanese, in particular when massive amounts of labour were required for some construction job. Otherwise, Chinese and Japanese were forced to enter and compete with the white job market, where they would in fact accept very low pay and thus threaten prevailing wage levels.

Instead of using its collective power to bring about higher minimum wages for all workers, whatever their racial origin, organized labour chose to view the mere presence of Chinese and Japanese as a threat. Trade union members often allied themselves with racist organizations like the White Canadian Association and the Asiatic Exclusion League. Concomitantly, British Columbia businessmen were not adverse to using Chinese and Japanese workers as tools in the long and bitter industrial struggles that characterized the early decades of this century. The deployment of Chinese and Japanese as strikebreakers especially aggravated an already tense situation.

Occasionally racial bitterness flared into open and devastating violence. Workers and union militants from Vancouver actively participated in the 1907 mob attacks on Chinese sections of the city that resulted in the burning and looting of Chinese properties. White workers on Vancouver Island rioted in 1913 when the mine owners began employing Chinese labourers as strikebreakers. Note also that until the World War II period, membership in all British Columbia craft unions remained closed to persons of Chinese or Japanese descent. This persistent exclusion from union membership was more subtle and less dramatic than labour strikes and other violent actions, but over the long term it probably caused greater damage to the Chinese and Japanese condition.

Chinese and Japanese in the prairie provinces had a somewhat easier time, since their smaller numbers reduced the apparent threat. To be sure, there were frequent cases of job discrimination in those areas, too, but by and large, direct competition with whites was low. Chinese in prairie towns generally opted for service-type employment in laundries or as domestics. Japanese in Alberta and Saskatchewan were scattered about as farm workers.

During the Depression years of the 1930s, doubts as to the wisdom of an anti-Oriental policy began to be felt in certain labour circles. In 1938, for instance, organized labour and its ally Co-operative Commonwealth Federation supported striking Chinese lime workers in a particularly violent strike at Blubber Bay, braving police repression in doing so.[49] When forced evacuation of the Japanese took place in World War II, British Columbia members of the CCF also displayed considerable courage in the face of public hysteria to protest the treatment of the evacuees.

Schooling and Housing

No specific discriminatory legislation was enacted affecting Chinese or Japanese education. The children were merely subject to the same rules and regulations that applied to all students in a province. Public schools were not segregated by law; *de facto* segregation simply reflected neighbourhood composition. On several occasions, however, groups of white parents did demand that Chinese and Japanese students be segregated from white pupils in the public schools. An investigation of some thirty-three public schools in Vancouver failed to substantiate the charges underlying these demands, and the Vancouver school board in 1914 refused to segregate the schools. Private schools also accepted Chinese and Japanese children, and on occasion Chinatown parents would choose to send their children to mission schools run by religious organizations.

In general there was considerable enthusiasm for education among the Chinese and Japanese, though sometimes of an ethnically particular kind. For example, in 1920 a Chinese Public School was founded in Calgary after a petition from the Chinese residents there. The school emphasized customs and values rather than providing the students with a diversified curriculum.[50]

The Japanese inaugurated a system of ethnic schools in 1906. Courses of instruction were mainly limited to reading and writing in the Japanese language. Occasionally Japanese history was taught also, using textbooks imported from Japan. Classes ranged from a few students meeting once or twice a week to 967 students meeting daily for two hours at the Alexander Street school in Vancouver.[51] By 1941, 59 Japanese-language schools were operating in British Columbia.

These language schools raised questions both without and within the Japanese community. Outside critics on the one hand contended that the classes conflicted with programs at the public schools and that they subversively spread Japanese nationalism. Within the Japanese community, on the other hand, there was considerable doubt about the schools' success. Most of the teachers were Japanese-born and trained and unable to speak English. Standards were low and salaries skimpy. Both students and teachers exhibited little enthusiasm. As a consequence, children often achieved only minimal fluency in either Japanese or English. Even so, the Japanese community struggled to maintain these schools over the years, thus illustrating the high symbolic value of language for perpetuating culture and traditions.

Few immigrant groups placed as much stress on education as did the Japanese. As is not uncommon, however, this heightened the conflict and distance between generations. In the teacher, the schools introduced an authority figure rivalling the father. The traditional male superiority was challenged. Older Japanese were torn between keeping their children like themselves or allowing them to advance in a new and vastly different society. Indeed, for years higher education was denied to girls because it might jeopardize a daughter's chance of marriage within the community.

A major problem for Japanese college graduates was job placement. The first Nisei to earn a degree from the University of British Columbia had to go to Alberta to find a teaching job. Even when local school boards were willing to employ a person of Japanese descent, pressures from the Parent Teacher Associations or from the Canadian Legion would force them to hire an Occidental. As economic conditions deteriorated in the 1930s Japanese college graduates found it all but impossible to find employment that would fit their training. To add insult to injury, after leaving a fairly liberal and open college environment, the Japanese graduates would return to their home communities and face overt discrimination in jobs, housing, and public accommodations. For example, in some Vancouver theatres Japanese were restricted to one side of the auditorium; the Parks Board of Vancouver restricted the use of Crystal Pool by Japanese to Tuesday mornings between 10:30 and 12:30; and Japanese were not allowed to use certain tennis courts.[52] The acceptance of employment in Issei-controlled businesses frequently posed problems, too, because of both lack of opportunity for advancement and conflicts between Issei owners and the college-trained Nisei.

One possible strategy for college-trained Japanese involved moving to eastern Canada. This movement, though small in numbers, became known as "The Great Adventure." It lasted from about 1936 to the outbreak of World War II. Those Nisei who did relocate encountered some opposition, but they were able to advance themselves and lay the groundwork for later migrations of Japanese Canadians after World War II.

Some parents tried to avoid these educational and occupational difficulties by sending their eldest child back to Japan for training. The experience gave the students fluency in the Japanese language and reinforced their Japanese temperament and personality. Some remained in Japan and did quite well in commerce and industry. Those that returned to Canada often faced problems similar to those that confronted the Issei generation.

The Chinese and Japanese both developed enclaves within cities. These "Chinatowns" and "Little Tokyos" were usually located near a waterfront or adjacent to core areas. Substandard rooming houses, apartments, and small businesses were centred there. As they acquired modest savings, however, some Chinese and Japanese moved into lower- and middle-income residential areas, especially if zoning regulations permitted them to establish businesses there. The general tendency was to form solid geographical concentrations. The resultant visibility fostered increased prejudice against the Chinese and Japanese. As prejudice increased, the degree of concentration increased in turn. Chinatown or Little Tokyo was a physical as well as a social fact. It reinforced traditional family systems, was a means of preserving and handing down cultures to succeeding generations, and provided a relatively secure haven in a hostile world.

A New Image
International developments over the years have greatly changed the image in Canada of Japan and of the Japanese people. In the early years of this century, Japan was considered weak and inferior to western nations. As it grew in industrial and military might, its ambitions turned toward the conquest of China, and later of the West. Hence it became a dangerous enemy. Following Japan's defeat in World War II it evolved into a democratic state politically, and a wealthy commercial and manufacturing nation economically.

Today Japan is considered a strong ally of Canada. High-quality products manufactured there fill Canadian stores. Canada has lucrative trading agreements with Japan. The establishment of subsidiaries by giant Japanese corporations is sought after by the same British Columbia that a generation ago talked of the "yellow peril." The Premier of the province and his cabinet ministers make highly publicized visits to Japan to encourage trade and investment, while other Canadian companies try to draw technical and managerial lessons from successful Japanese enterprises. Not surprisingly, antiquated notions of Japanese racial inferiority are a chief casualty of this change, and Japanese Canadians are being accepted on a far more humane and egalitarian basis than in the past.

This is not to imply, however, that the Japanese community in Vancouver has ever regained its pre-eminence and élan. Many of the traditional community leaders are not only aging but also lack the power and influence to bridge the gaps between generations. Their values of filial piety, honour, and moral obligation no longer seem so relevant, especially given the World War II internment experiences. These cultural norms also fail to touch many recent immigrants, given their upbringing in the educationally and socially transformed Japan of the post-1945 era. Indeed, while the Issei (and to an extent the Nisei) tended to be collectively oriented, the newer Japanese arrivals are predominantly individualistic in their social outlook.

Moreover, many of the Japanese who were evacuated from the West Coast during World War II never found it in their hearts to return. Instead, some settled permanently in the prairies, not far from where the internment camps had been. They began by working the farms of others. Now many have their own farms and are an accepted part of agricultural communities in Alberta and Saskatchewan. Tom Ohara, former "world potato king" began growing potatoes on thirty-five rented acres in 1943, and owned fifteen hundred acres by 1970.[53] Other Japanese have gone into agricultural research and contributed to improving potato and sugar beet production.

Some Nisei have entered politics on local levels as members of town councils, mainly in Alberta and the interior of British Columbia. A few former evacuees have even attained positions of leadership in the generalized Alberta social system. For example, Dr. James Oshiro, a physician, was named Chancellor of the University of Lethbridge. This marked the first time a Japanese Canadian had been appointed to such a position.[54] Dr. Robert Miyagishima, another physician, was one of three surgeons who took part in Toronto's first heart transplant. Architect Raymond Moriyama, designer of Toronto's Japanese Canadian Cultural Centre, was the site-planner for the Ontario Science Centre, the Scarborough Civic Centre, and Metro Toronto's new zoo.

Immigration, too, is once again affecting Japanese demography in Canada. Their high level of technical skills and education has gained them easy acceptance as immigrants to Canada. In 1966, a visa office was opened in Tokyo, and a vigorous advertising campaign launched in order to attract highly qualified technical and professional prospects. A one-month intensive English language training course was offered there to ease the transition to life in Canada. The success of these efforts was evident in the subsequent three-fold increase in Japanese immigration.[55]

Numbers, however, remain small. Certainly, few Japanese enter compared with Chinese. Since World War II, Japanese yearly immigration has ranged from a low of just two in 1947 to a high of only 1,020 in 1973.[56] This contrasts with the 14,465 Chinese who officially arrived that same year from Hong Kong, the People's Republic of China, and Taiwan.

Postwar Japanese immigration has primarily been directed toward Toronto rather then Vancouver. Indeed, the Japanese population of Metropolitan Toronto considerably exceeds that of Vancouver and its environs. The fact that the Japanese Canadian Cultural Centre has been established in Toronto rather than on the West Coast is just one more reflection of this changing distribution.

In the late nineteenth century, Japanese immigration was a response to the demand for cheap labour by the Canadian economy. Government policy, therefore, did not stress educational skills. The immigrants tended to understand no English on arrival and to learn little of it during their years of residence. They relied heavily on community social organizations such as the Japanese Canadian Citizens Association, the Japanese Property Owners Association, the Camp and Mill Workers Union, and the Canadian Japanese Association for defence against discrimination and for moral and material support in times of unemployment or other crisis.

By contrast, the new immigrants are more self-sufficient. They meet the skill criteria of the current point system. They are usually well educated, and many are college graduates. Many are bilingual. Some 30 percent may be occupationally categorized as professional, mechanical, or managerial. For all these reasons, recent Japanese immigrants usually feel that they do not need the support of community organizations in order to find jobs or ward off prejudice. They can rely on their own individual merit.

Chinese Continuities

The Chinese in Canada have never reached as high or low a point as the Japanese. Traditionally the Chinese fared less well than the Japanese, and many more federal regulations and provincial laws were passed against them. Yet even with the disappearance of these measures, the Chinese have not achieved the same level of prosperity enjoyed by the Japanese.

While the Chinese Immigration Act of 1923 was repealed in 1947, the only Chinese allowed to enter until 1952 were those whose family members were Canadian residents. Now, the gates are open considerably wider. As noted above, nearly fifteen thousand Chinese were recorded as arriving in the single year of 1973 alone. Most came from Hong Kong, though many were refugees from the Communist China mainland.

Some of these Chinese, and others who slipped into the country uncounted, were illegal immigrants, their entry facilitated through purchased documents, bribery, and phony relatives. In order to legalize their presence in Canada, a Chinese Adjustment Statement Program was begun in 1960. Modelled after the American Truthful Statement Program for Chinese, in effect since 1956, it called upon Chinese who had entered Canada illegally to present themselves and make complete and honest statements about the circumstances under which they came into the country, together with truthful information on their family backgrounds. In return, the illegal entrants would have their cases reviewed by the Minister of Citizenship and Immigration, and might be permitted to remain. Between June 1960 and July 1970, 11,569 Chinese had their status adjusted.[57]

Some sons and grandsons of Chinese immigrants have entered the professions. Dr. Wah Leung became Dean of Dentistry at the University of British Columbia. Peter Wing served as mayor of Kamloops, British

Columbia from 1965 to 1972. Douglas Jung was elected M.P. from Vancouver in 1956.[58] But the immediate prospects of most Chinese still seem ambiguous. As an illustration, consider the future of their "Chinatowns." On the one hand, the importance of these areas as centres of Chinese culture, business, and residence has been declining. "As Chinese have gained access to the political, legal, occupational and social positions once open only to Caucasians, they have drifted away from Chinatown, losing interest in its insular institutions, and shutting themselves off from its benefits and influence."[59] On the other hand, there continues to be reluctance, among new Chinese as well as old, to abandon these enclaves entirely. Chinese in a number of cities have made national headlines because of their resistance to urban renewal schemes that would have destroyed these neighbourhoods.

A Final Word

Official statements and actions indicative of deep racial prejudice against Chinese and Japanese abounded throughout the hundred years that separate the mid-1800s from the mid-1900s. Even immediately following World War II they were easy to find. But now, and for the past twenty years or so, government policies toward racial and ethnic minorities have changed. The perpetuation of such cultures is being encouraged and supported.

How far such official changes imply a fundamental reorientation in public attitudes is open to question. A television interviewer has little trouble locating Canadians who volubly claim that things have gone too far, the doors of immigration have been flung open too wide, and that some of those people ought to be sent back where they came from. Sociologists can also readily uncover new symptoms of racial tension and violence in the public schools. This dread, however, appears to be principally focused on immigrants with brown or black skins.[60]

As far as Chinese and Japanese specifically are concerned, the inveterate fears and prejudices expressed by the white majority are on the wane. At the same time, the economic and social conditions of the Chinese and Japanese have changed massively for the better. These two developments are closely linked. Greater acceptance by the majority facilitates socio-economic improvements. The improvements in turn provide the way for readier acceptance.

NOTES

[1] Adachi, Ken, *The Enemy That Never Was* (Toronto: McClelland and Stewart Ltd., 1976), p. 67.

[2] *Canada Year Book 1975*, Statistics Canada (Ottawa: Information Canada, 1975), p. 169.

[3] Baureiss, Gunter, "The Chinese Community in Calgary," *Alberta Historical Review*, 22:2, Spring 1974, p. 2.

[4] Morton, James, *In the Sea of Sterile Mountains* (Vancouver: J. J. Douglas, 1973), p. 138.

[5] *Ibid.*, p. 123.

[6] *Ibid.*, p. 122.

[7] *Ibid.*, p. 122.

[8] Cheng, Tien-Fang, *Oriental Immigration in Canada* (Shanghai: The Commercial Press Ltd., 1931), p. 255.

[9] Morton, *op. cit.*, p. 220.

[10] *Statutes of Canada*, 1903, c. 8.

[11] Kung, S. W., "Chinese Immigration into North America," *Queen's Quarterly*, 68:4, Winter 1962, pp. 612 and 616.

[12] Baureiss, *op. cit.*, p. 3.

[13] *Ibid.*, p. 8.

[14] *Ibid.*, p. 3. By 1921, the Chinese population had risen to 688, the white population to 63,305.

[15] Adachi, *op. cit.*, p. 9.

[16] *Ibid.*, p. 87.

[17] Young, Charles Y., and Helen R. Y. Reid, *The Japanese Canadians* (Toronto: University of Toronto Press, 1938), p. 107.

[18] Adachi, *op. cit.*, p. 102.

[19] *Ibid.*, p. 188.

[20] *Ibid.*, p. 234.

[21] LaViolette, Forrest E., *The Japanese Canadians* (Toronto: Canadian Institute of International Affairs, 1945), p. 1.

[22] Adachi, *op. cit.*, p. 235.

[23] LaViolette, Forrest E., *The Canadian Japanese and World War II* (Toronto: University of Toronto Press, 1948), p. 153.

[24] Marx, Herbert, "The Emergency Power and Civil Liberties in Canada," *McGill Law Journal*, 16:1, March 1970, p. 78.

[25] *Ibid.*, p. 79.

[26] See further, Chapter 8.

[27] To be discussed in a second volume of our study.

[28] LaViolette, *op. cit.*, *The Canadian Japanese and World War II*, p. 44.

[29] Marx, *op. cit.*, p. 86.

[30] *Globe and Mail*, October 28, 1968, p. 12.

[31] Adachi, *op. cit.*, p. 287.

[32] Quoted in Adachi, *op. cit.*, p. 366.

[33] Woodsworth, James S., *Strangers Within Our Gates* (Toronto: University of Toronto Press, reprinted 1972), p. 154.

[34] *House of Commons Debates, Session 1922*, Vol. II, p. 1513.

[35] *Canada, House of Commons Debates*, Vol. 3, 1947, pp. 2644-47.

[36] Cited in Freda Hawkins, *Canada and Immigration* (Montreal: McGill-Queen's University Press, 1972), p. 85.

[37] (1903) *Appeals Court* 151, at p. 157. Recall also the question of Chinese hair styles mentioned earlier in this chapter.

[38] *Revised Statutes of British Columbia*, 1936, c. 228.

[39] Corbett, David C., *Canada's Immigration Policy* (Toronto: University of Toronto Press, 1957), p. 77.

[40] *Statutes of Ontario, 1914*, c. 40.

[41] *Statutes of Quebec, 1915*, c. 22.

[42] *Statutes of British Columbia, 1875*, No. 2; *1895*, c. 20, s. 2; and *1896*, c. 38.

[43] Berton, Pierre, *The National Dream: The Great Railway, 1871-1881* (Toronto: McClelland and Stewart Ltd., 1970), p. 189.

[44] *Cunningham v. Tomey-Homma, (1903) Appeals Court* 151; *Quong Wing v. The King (1914)*, 49 S. C. R., 440.

[45] *Statutes of British Columbia, 1899*, c. 39, s. 36; *Rules of the Law Society of British Columbia*, No. 39; *Pharmacy By-Laws*, Section 15.

[46] *Statutes of Canada, 1920*, c. 46, s. 36 (G).

[47] The Japanese Retired Soldiers Association spent many years lobbying in favour of provincial voting privileges for Japanese war veterans. Not until 1931 did British Columbia grant them the vote, and by that time it benefited fewer than eighty men.

[48] *Canada Sessional Papers*, No. 29, p. 53; *British Columbia Public Works Contract*, clause 45; Young and Reid, *The Japanese Canadians*, p. 130; *Statutes of British Columbia*, 1925, c. 32.

[49] Phillips, Paul, *No Power Greater: A Century of Labour in British Columbia* (Vancouver: British Columbia Federation of Labour, 1967), pp.116-17.

[50] Baureiss, *op. cit.*, p. 7.

[51] Adachi, *op. cit.*, p. 128.

[52] *Ibid.*, p. 172.

[53] *Ibid.*, p. 359.

[54] Iwaasa, David B., "The Japanese in Southern Alberta," *Alberta History*, 24:3, Summer 1976, p. 18.

[55] Ujimoto, K. Victor, "Contrasts in the Prewar and Postwar Japanese Community in British Columbia: Conflict and Change," *Canadian Review of Sociology and Anthropology*, 13:1, February 1976, p. 85.

[56] *1974 Immigration Statistics* (Canada, Manpower and Immigration) (Ottawa: Information Canada, 1975), p. 6.

[57] Hawkins, *op. cit.*, p. 133.

[58] Morton, *op. cit.*, p. 255.

[59] Lyman, Stanford M., "Chinese Secret Societies in the Occident," *Canadian Review of Sociology and Anthropology*, 1:2, May 1964, p. 100.

[60] For Blacks, see Chapter 4; for Asian Indians, see Chapter 6; for Mexicans, see Appendix.

Chapter 6
OTHER ASIANS AND MIGRATORY WORKERS

Of necessity, the present chapter is more diverse than those that preceded it. Two separate time periods are examined: the first ends at World War II; the second follows it. For the first period we briefly examine such by-now-familiar topics as immigration restrictions, franchise denial, and employment problems. For the second we canvass such themes as the Commonwealth connection (as viewed from both Canada and India), the new tensions, and brain drains.

Diversity is also unavoidable because of the variety of peoples involved. "Other Asians" includes populations from Pakistan eastward, encompassing India, Bangladesh, Nepal, Sri Lanka, Indonesia, Vietnam, and the Philippines, as well as transplanted Asians from countries like Kenya and Uganda. An appendix to this chapter also touches upon migratory workers, primarily those from Mexico and the Caribbean.

Terminology is a problem. Words like "Oriental" and "Asiatic" have deprecatory overtones. "Indian," without modification, is ambiguous. "East Indian" is reminiscent of the old name for Indonesia. "Hindu" and "Sikh" are inaccurate, as they refer to religious rather than racial distinctions and apply to just two of many such affiliations that characterize Asia. In addition, many lands have been freed only in the last thirty years from their colonial, often British, masters. Independence sometimes meant fission. Imperial India was partitioned in 1948 to create India and Pakistan, with East Pakistan officially becoming Bangladesh in 1974. Countries may change their name, too, as Ceylon did in opting to be called Sri Lanka.

The trouble is not merely that words are slippery, but that it is often difficult to know where one is at. How many Asians were there in Canada on a given census date? Ambiguities in nomenclature and a tendency to lump these people in overall or residual categories like "Other Asian," "Australasian," or, "not otherwise specified," make it impossible to answer the question.

In recent years the count has become more detailed, creating the opportunity to say something valid about the particular countries of origin. During 1974 alone, 12,868 persons from India were admitted into the country, along with 158 from Bangladesh, 2,843 from South Korea, 213 from Indonesia, 2,315 from Pakistan, 527 from Sri Lanka, 9,564 from the

Philippines, and 373 from South Vietman.[1] In each instance, the majority of the new immigrants settled in Ontario.

Early Immigration

The first East Indians to visit British Columbia were members of Sikh regiments passing through Canada in 1897 on their way home from Queen Victoria's Diamond Jubilee celebration in England.[2] East Indians were the third category of people from the Orient, after the Chinese and Japanese, to enter British Columbia. From the start, they were often viewed as unacceptable by the white population. Their mere presence, it was thought, constituted a problem. Indeed, the "Hindu problem" was "the most recent and in some ways the most difficult of all. . . . Their standards of living and manner of life and thought are far different from ours. However estimable they may be in India, they are sadly out of place in Canada.[3]

The situation became more serious in September 1907, when some seven hundred East Indians who had been expelled from Seattle and surrounding American communities crossed the border into British Columbia. In swift reaction, the Asiatic Exclusion League organized a parade to Vancouver City Hall. This in turn precipitated a series of riots in the city's Chinatown area as well as its Japanese and East Indian quarters.[4] Blame for the riot was placed on the Seattle Exclusion League and other American organizations. The federal government reimbursed the Japanese for property losses. Chinese and East Indians were not reimbursed.

Various discouraging rules that applied primarily to Chinese and Japanese tended to inhibit the immigration of other Asians as well. For example, they were required to have at least two hundred dollars in their possession upon arrival. From 1909 onward, they also had to reach Canada via a single continuous passage. This latter requisite particularly militated against Asian Indians, since few ships sailed directly between India and Canada.[5] At some point in their journey, in the Philippines or Hawaii or elsewhere, these people would have had to stop and transfer to another vessel.

With the adoption of the "gentlemen's agreement" limiting Japanese immigration, a drastic decline in the number of East Indians entering Canada also occurred. Whereas 2,623 East Indians had been admitted in 1908, in 1910 only 5 were permitted entry; in 1911, 37; in 1912, 3.[6] Moreover, the three latter groups came by "continuous passage" and were actually former British Columbians who had already established Canadian domicile and had been visiting their native homeland.

In 1913, 36 East Indians arrived in Vancouver aboard a ship from Singapore. They were served deportation notices by an immigration officer. The East Indians took their case to court, asking for a writ of *habeas corpus* on the grounds that they were being illegally detained pending deportation. Justice Dennis Murphy of the British Columbia Supreme Court dismissed the application, stating that he could not interfere with an Immigration Act since it was a federal statute. The East Indians then appealed to the Chief Justice of that court, Gordon Hunter, who ordered the men released on the basis that they were British citizens. To resolve the dilemma, the federal government issued new orders making it illegal for labourers, skilled or unskilled, to enter Canada at any port in British Columbia.[7]

The restrictions on East Indian immigration were tested even more severely a year later. On May 23, 1914 a steamer, the *Komagata Maru* arrived in Vancouver with 376 East Indian Sikhs on board. The ship had been chartered for both financial and political reasons by a Punjabi agitator, Gurdit Singh. The East Indians were not permitted to disembark, and the ship lay at anchor in Vancouver harbour until July 23. Case after case involving the ship and its owner were brought before the British Columbia courts. Living conditions aboard the vessel were deplorable. Rations were soon exhausted and the shipping company refused to supply more. At times there was not even drinking water available. A riot on board took the lives of twenty men. After months of litigation, the ship left harbour under Canadian naval escort and returned to India with its human cargo.[8]

Despite the immigration restrictions and the opposition from white Canadians, some East Indians did continue to enter British Columbia. These people were mainly uneducated and unskilled. Most lived in small enclaves within South Vancouver and other British Columbia cities. A comparative handful migrated to the prairie provinces, where they worked as farm hands or in lumber mills.

As more Chinese and East Asians came to British Columbia, a corresponding increase occurred in the number of racist organizations there. In addition to the Asiatic Exclusion League, which at one time claimed a membership of forty thousand, there existed the White Canada Association, the United Farmers of British Columbia, the Great War Veterans Association, the Orange Order, as well as others at the local level.[9] Skin tone and cultural patterns were targets for most of these groups; the Orange Order also questioned and criticized the religious practices of the East Indians.

The Franchise

In strict law, Asian Indians were not aliens but British subjects, eligible to become Canadian citizens in the same way as other British subjects, to vote, and to hold office. In actuality, they suffered disabilities little different from those of the Chinese and Japanese. Within British Columbia, they were not allowed to participate in elections at all. Though rarely referred to by name in legislation, they were usually ensnared by some phrase or term it included.

For example, a law could be amended or extended to include "Other Asians" or "Other Orientals." In this way, the 1875 disenfranchisement of the Chinese in British Columbia was made applicable to all British Columbia Asians twenty years later.[10] Moreover, once East Indians could no longer be placed on voters' lists, they were also unable to apply for various licences. As an illustration, none of them could receive a logger's licence for work in the lumber industry.

Clearly, racial antipathies were at work. White persons of British nationality could vote in British Columbia; non-white Asian persons who were British subjects could not. As a result of the federal Franchise Act of 1920, they could not vote in federal elections either.[11] The situation in British Columbia was not rectified until 1947. Nowadays, all Asians who are naturalized Canadians or were born in this country can participate in elections.

Employment

Because of their small numbers, in comparison with the Chinese or Japanese, Asian Indians who arrived early did not pose a major threat to white workers. In addition, they lacked national organizations and avoided conspicuous protest. As a result they were usually allowed to eke out a living as unskilled help in the fishing or lumbering industries.

In the 1920s and 1930s, however, white Canadians found new reasons for fearing the Asians. The United States had ended its policy of free immigration and instituted a quota system; this, it was felt, could mean trouble for Canada. The reason for apprehension lay in partial blockage of the emigrant flow from Canada to the United States. Before the 1920s, new arrivals in Canada had been as free as native Canadians to move south of the border. Indeed, the assumption made was that the stream of immigrants from Canada to the United States had been of the same composition as the total Canadian community. But now that was bound to change.

Native-born Canadians remained free to cross into the States. Immigrants living in Canada, by contrast, had to wait until they could find an opening within the quota of their country of origin. Consequently, many white "English" Canadians would be replaced by new "non-English" Canadians to whom the exit southward was closed. The possible consequences of this worried "the man in the street;" and was elaborated upon by academics.

A displacement theory of migration was proffered by Canadian economists of the 1930s. It suggested that low-paid immigrants to Canada would compete for scarce jobs with residents demanding a higher standard of living. The immigrants would get the jobs. Residents would have to move down to the States where they could obtain better work at better pay.[12] Therefore the ethnic composition of Canada would alter drastically, a prospect that haunted many Canadians through the decade.

The Commonwealth Connection

A new look in governmental policy toward Asian immigration revealed itself in the early 1950s. Agreements were reached with the governments of India, Pakistan, and Ceylon, permitting 150 Indians, 100 Pakistanis, and 50 Ceylonese to be admitted into Canada each year. In addition, wives, husbands, unmarried children under twenty-one, fathers over sixty-five, and mothers over sixty of Canadian citizens, resident in Canada, from these three countries of origin would be allowed to enter.[13] Immigration offices were opened in New Delhi (1952) and Islamabad, Pakistan (1967), as well as in three other non-Commonwealth Asian cities.

There is little question that the sustaining of Commonwealth ties weighed heavily in these decisions. Asked in 1955 why a staff of twelve was required in New Delhi to process the 150 Indians who would be accepted yearly, J. W. Pickersgill, then Minister of Citizenship and Immigration, responded:

> As a matter of fact, you know as well as I do, that we do not have an office in India for the purpose of getting immigrants, for the sake of increasing the population of Canada. We agreed upon this quota as a gesture for the improvement of Commonwealth relations. And, having done so, we have to treat these applicants decently and have enough employees there to answer the letters and deal with the correspondence and the applications which are received.[14]

And, in fact, the staff had a fair amount of work to do, since some twenty thousand applications were soon received.

Before 1962, Canada's official attitude toward Asian immigration was racially based, though the notion "race" was bent far out of its ordinary anthropological shape. For, to the extent that any scientific worth inheres in classifying peoples racially, Asiatic Indians would usually be considered Nordics, often darker in hue than most Europeans but possessing rather similar facial and bodily features.[15] Certainly, native leaders in the Indian subcontinent have long bridled at British (and Western) colour prejudices. Their resentment fueled the fires of nationalism prior to and during World War II. And the removal of such discriminatory practices abroad has continued to be a major external goal for both India and Pakistan.

Racial bias in the treatment of East Indians throughout the Commonwealth hardly disappeared with the independence of India and Pakistan. Large numbers of overseas East Indians—about three million all told—were living in places like Jamaica, Trinidad, Kenya, Tanzania, Uganda, and British Guiana. Many of them, or their forebears, had originally arrived as cheap unskilled labour, often indentured, but they usually remained after their term of service was complete. Even so, they rarely became assimilated into the general population of the host country, and instead retained their native language, religion, and social practices. They were later sometimes joined by other East Indians, unbound by indenture, who sought their fortune as traders or labourers. Though some prospered materially and were able to see that their children became well-educated, all tended to live as second-class citizens, with their rights of voting and property ownership closely restricted.

These people looked to the government of India for protection of their civil rights, and that government accepted the responsibility. It considered as Indians even those whose families had left India two and three generations back, and it conducted negotiations on their behalf. Such efforts have, however, been relatively fruitless in East Africa.

The crises that arose there ultimately had a direct effect upon Canada itself. The problem took about a decade in coming to a head. When Kenya and Uganda received independence in the early 1960s, Asians living there were given the choice of taking Kenyan (Ugandan) or United Kingdom citizenship. Most opted for the latter. This was probably an unwise decision as the African governments soon began confining occupational licences to their own citizens, and many Indians who had by now often entered trades, merchandizing, and the professions needed such permits to carry on business.

When these Asian Indians wished to leave Africa for Britain or India, they found that their passports gained them automatic entry to neither country. India, which was already repatriating nationals from Ceylon and Burma, would not willingly absorb them and began requiring visa approval. Britain, fearing further racial unrest, passed legislation which deviated from the principle of free Commonwealth immigration. The crisis became more acute in 1972, when the President of Uganda, Idi Amin, announced that all members of the Asian minority would be expelled from the country in a few months. Even those few Asians who had acquired Ugandan nationality faced the prospect of being made stateless.

When the British government appealed to Canada for assistance, Canada's reaction was prompt and positive. Indeed, apart from Britain itself, Canada ultimately received more Ugandan Asians than all other countries combined. To facilitate the medical examination of the applicants, a mobile laboratory of the Canadian Armed Forces was flown from Canada to Kampala. From September 5 to November 8, 1972 over six thousand Asians obtained immigrant visas on the spot. Chartered airplanes flew the refugees directly from Kampala to Montreal. Altogether, 4,420 persons were airlifted to Canada in 31 flights. While in transit, the refugees were given job counselling, winter clothing, and pocket money if needed.[16]

In 1973 over two thousand additional Ugandans came into Canada, and 423 in 1974.[17] Altogether, over seven thousand Ugandan Asians are now living in Canada. They have been encouraged to settle widely throughout the country in order to ease housing and job pressures and to help speed their integration within the larger social order. Unemployment is low, though a few people are still enrolled in Manpower Training Programs. Remarkably few difficulties were encountered in the resettlement, which cost about four million dollars.

Canada has participated in refugee programs for non-Commonwealth Asians also. Thus, the federal government advised the exiled Dalai Lama that it would accept a limited number of Tibetans. A group of families and single adults and their spiritual leaders, some 228 persons in all, were settled in Canada. By agreement with the provinces concerned, they were distributed among rural areas of Ontario, Quebec, Manitoba, Saskatchewan, and Alberta. Coming from a vastly different environment and culture, the Tibetans needed extra assistance. Costs proved relatively high for the program, in part at least because these refugees were unskilled and their initial unemployment rate was high. Most of these people have now completed courses in language and basic skills and are gainfully employed.

With the impending Communist victory over in South Vietnam, Canada admitted 418 South Vietnamese in 1973 and 373 in 1974. During those same two years, 1,553 and then 2,843 South Koreans also entered Canada. Most of these people are employed on farms in the prairie provinces. Due to political strife in the Philippines, the number of persons from there seeking admission into Canada has been increasing markedly. In 1973 6,757 Filipinos came into the country, and 9,564 in 1974.[18]

The New Tensions

East Asians who have recently immigrated to Canada have been targets of racially motivated attacks, primarily in Vancouver and Toronto. In part this may be because of their education and technical skills placing them in a strong position to compete with white Canadians for jobs which are already scarce in the current economic situation. In any event, often refusing to fight back for religious reasons, Indians and Pakistanis have suffered physical attacks on subways, schoolyard harassments, and destruction of their community religious centres. In one Toronto incident, a Tanzanian immigrant was pushed off a subway platform by three drunken white youths and permanently disabled as a result. Several times the police have been accused of providing inadequate protection for the East Indians, even though there had been prior warning of the attack. In reaction, the usually pacifist East Indians are talking of defending themselves against violence by forming vigilante groups.[19]

Rather similar incidents have marked the increased immigration of East Indians into West Coast cities. In 1971, obscenities were painted on the walls of South Vancouver's Sikh Temple, the largest structure of its kind outside India.[20] White youth gangs have hunted down and assaulted East Indians on the streets of Surrey, North Vancouver, and Burnaby.

Children of Asian immigrants attend public as well as private schools. One of the biggest problems is in the area of language. Some groups, such as the Koreans, read and write English fairly well, though they may have difficulty speaking it. For other Asians, the language problems are even more pervading.

Asian cultural traits, directly or indirectly, have a variety of impacts on the educational experience. For example, East Indian girls are generally passive and non-questioning in the classroom, while the boys are more aggressive and outgoing. Asian children have often been subjected to name-calling, bullying, and harassment in the schools, particularly within British Columbia. Sikh students in particular are taunted for wearing turbans and for their style of dress.

Efforts in Great Britain to develop English-language skills among East Indians have included a system of home tutoring by volunteer teachers. This approach is now being tried in Vancouver and other Canadian cities. It is too early to evaluate the program, but clearly the road is not an easy one. In general there has been little enthusiasm for these programs. Many mothers work; in other cases cultural attitudes keep women out of the classes; capable volunteer teachers may be difficult to find. And besides, most school systems do not have the funding for such a program. These types of language programs would benefit the mothers and would help close the educational gap between parent and child.

A more ambitious effort in Vancouver, this time aimed at younger people, makes use of public school facilities over the summer months. The Khalsa-Diwan Society of the Sikh Temple, members of the Vancouver School Board, the Metropolitan Health Board, and personnel from the University of British Columbia operate a summer school program for children of various ethnic groups. Of the 112 children enrolled in 1971, 70 were East Asians. Interim measures of success called for the program's continuation on an annual basis.[21]

A Brain Drain?

At the end of World War II, there were in the Indian subcontinent some 18 universities as well as 115 professional schools in fields such as law, medicine, teaching, engineering, and agriculture. There were about

4,200 high schools. Just over 5 percent of the population was then liter-ate. By 1966, figures for the nation of India alone (i.e., not counting East and West Pakistan) included 80 universities, 1,940 arts and science col-leges, 386 medical and veterinary colleges, and many other institutions in science, engineering, and technology. Many young people from India were also studying abroad. The literacy rate in 1971 stood at nearly 30 percent.[22]

Like several other Western countries, Canada particularly welcomes the highly educated and skilled immigrant. These are the attributes that the current point system singles out for approbation. Sometimes, to be sure, the reception is a bit less than totally enthusiastic. Immigrants may, for example, have to take further studies to upgrade their qualifica-tions before being accorded recognition in Canada. In other cases, em-ployers insist upon prior "Canadian experience." These inhibitions are most evident in medical and health professions, architecture, teaching, social work, and some technical trades[23], but they are not so severe as to dissuade the educated from immigrating. A survey made in 1974 in Met-ropolitan Toronto highlights the impressive educational experience that newcomers from Asia often bring with them.[24]

In general, the flow of highly trained individuals from developing to developed countries—e.g., from India to Canada—enriches the latter at the expense of the former. Moreover, as Hawkins notes, "The most serious loss sustained by the developing countries may be the one which is most difficult to measure: that is, the loss of political and managerial talent and of men and women of vigour and enterprise whatever their professions and skills may be."[25] A study conducted by the Commission on International Development, and chaired by former Prime Minister Lester B. Pearson, also saw the problem as one of serious proportions. As it indicated, the present flow of skilled, qualified personnel from poor to rich countries actually exceeds that of advisory personnel from rich to poor countries.[26]

Stating this specifies facts but does not necessarily assign blame. The Canadian government has been sensitive to its responsibilities, and con-ducts no active recruitment programs in developing countries. Some of the skilled Asians are refugees from Kenya and Uganda, unable or un-willing to return to India. Students from Asia who are enrolled in Cana-dian institutions, and especially those who receive financial assistance from the Canadian government must sign a pledge at the outset to re-turn to their home country. Certainly there is no official enticement for them to remain.

Other mitigating circumstances may be mentioned. Entire families are now admitted into the country, not just talented individuals. In recent years more than half the immigrants have, in fact, been women, chil-dren, and older parents, none of whom are destined to contribute to the immediate job market. In addition, some immigrants either remain in

Canada only temporarily, usually moving on to the United States, or replace other personnel who have made a similar journey southward. None of these considerations, however, reduce the deleterious effect that the "brain drain" can have on developing countries. Even without intent—or with the best of intentions—Canada's immigration policy can hurt these countries.

Appendix

A NOTE ON MIGRATORY WORKERS

Despite increasing mechanization of farms, the use of temporary, seasonal workers in agriculture is becoming more prevalent among all major food producing countries. The term "migratory workers" is commonly applied in Canada and the United States, while in countries of the European Common Market these workers are referred to as "guest workers." Migratory workers usually arrive with their immediate families, while guest workers are either single or come alone.

Canadian migratory workers come from Portugal, the West Indies, and (especially) Mexico. Many have entered illegally, though the federal government has been tightening its control procedures at all border points. The magnitude of the illegal entrant problem was at least partially revealed in 1973, when about fifteen thousand persons were newly classified as immigrants under a special federal program to legalize the status of unauthorized residents.[27] At about the same time the right of subsequent migratory workers to change their status after arrival to "immigrant" was withdrawn. Visitors, including migratory workers, who seek temporary entry for more than three months must now first register with immigration officials outside Canada. Non-immigrants who are coming to work for more limited periods must obtain employment visas.

Migratory workers and their families experience most of the usual problems of immigrants, along with special ones deriving from their transitory condition. Schooling for children is almost non-existent. Living conditions are often degrading and pay rates low. Deficiencies of this sort were revealed in 1973 by a federal task force from the Ministry of Manpower and Immigration, which surveyed problems of seasonal migrants in Ontario and Quebec. The task force uncovered many instances of children, sick adults, and pregnant women working in fields harvesting crops. In some cases, while all members of a migrant family had to work, only the head of the household would receive any pay for his labour. In Quebec, one family of ten worked in the fields for a total weekly income of $60. Most migrant housing was clearly substandard and lacked sanitary facilities.

In addition, brokers were sometimes used to recruit farm labourers at a fee of $500 per head. The fee in turn was usually deducted from the worker's earnings. Mexicans were also frequently expected to pay their own transportation costs into and out of Canada, though the trucks carrying them often originated in Canada.[28]

In summer 1973, the federal government inaugurated a new set of priorities covering temporary work. Canadians are to be given preference. If Canadian workers are unavailable, second choice goes to those who are part of organized and approved movements like the Caribbean Seasonal Workers Program. As a last resort, individual foreigners with proper employment visas will be allowed to take the jobs.

The Caribbean Seasonal Workers Program is itself structured by agreements between Canada and the governments of some Caribbean countries: Jamaica, Barbados, Trinidad, and Tobago. The agreements cover recruitment of agricultural workers, their weekly guaranteed minimum wage, their accommodations, and transportation. Canadian employers notify a Canada Manpower Centre of their needs. If the demand cannot be met domestically, messages are relayed to the particular island governments, which then recruit the workers. Specific contracts between the Canadian employer and the workers follow. Liaison officers from each country involved are stationed in Canada to resolve complaints by either workers or employers and to help with transportation arrangements; the Canadian government contributes to the cost of these officers. During 1973, over three thousand workers came to Canada under this program. Only 140 were repatriated before the end of their contract; and fewer than 100 cases of breaches of contract were reported.[29]

In order to make better use of Canadian and landed immigrant workers and perhaps to save taxpayers money, the federal government has created a system of Canada Farm Labour Pools which are affiliated with Canada Manpower Centres. These pools may result in lower numbers of migratory workers coming to Canada. Even so, in June 1974 an agreement was signed with Mexico that regulates the flow of migratory workers from that country, and guarantees improvement in their treatment in Canada. Mexican nationals aged eighteen or over and destined for harvesting jobs in Canada will now be recruited by the Mexican government, paid a standard weekly wage, and have their transportation and living expenses partially subsidized by the farmers hiring them.

For employers, the advantage in having a ready supply of labour over short periods is obvious. This is especially true in fruit, vegetable, and tobacco farming, where growing and harvesting are concentrated in a few summer months. For the migratory workers, there is the advantage of earning a larger income or any income at all. Various disadvantages, however, also abound. Migratory workers, principally through payroll income tax reductions, pay for certain social services from which they rarely benefit. They can make little use of educational facilities, and health insurance benefits are not available to them. Nor, despite paying premiums, are they eligible for unemployment insurance payments.

A Comparative Comment

Firm data on Asians (apart from Chinese and Japanese) and on migratory workers in present-day Canada have yet to be collected. What is known, though, seems both sensible and suggestive. Currently, East Indians and other immigrants from Asia reap advantages from legality of residence, relatively large numbers, urban concentration, settled housing, educational attainment, job skills, and developed association. Not every Asian individual, or Asian community, scores high on every one of these considerations, but at least until recently the gulf between them and migratory workers has been clear. In general, such workers in Canada have been plagued by illegality of status, small populations scattered about in rural areas, transitory living conditions, little or no formal education, a lack of employable sophistication, and either no vocal leaders at all or the sort of leadership that sells the ordinary worker out in a sweetheart contract, that is, for a set price negotiates a contract that is not in the best interests of the workers.

The gap is now narrowing considerably. In part, this may be due to a greater humanitarian concern for migrants among federal and provincial authorities. An even greater share of the explanation lies in the active intervention of their home governments as spelled out in the provisions of the various treaties involving Mexico and the Caribbean nations. Parity in the position of migratory workers with Asian immigrants, however, is hardly to be expected. For in the nature of things, these comparatively seasonal visitors are destined to remain far less fixed in their abode, far less urbanized, and far less educated. Such characteristics seem sure to preclude their obtaining the advantages that political influence can often bring about.

NOTES

1 *Immigration '74, Fourth Quarter,* Manpower and Immigration (Ottawa: Information Canada, 1975), p. 4.

2 Ferguson, Ted, *A White Man's Country* (Toronto: Doubleday Canada, 1975), p. 3.

3 Woodsworth, James S., *Strangers Within Our Gates* (Toronto: University of Toronto Press, reprinted 1972), p. 154.

4 Ormsby, Margaret A., *British Columbia: A History* (Vancouver: The Macmillan Company of Canada Ltd., 1958), p. 350.

5 Boggs, Theodore H., "The Oriental on the Pacific Coast," *Queen's Quarterly,* 33:3, January 1926, p. 318.

6 Ferguson, *op. cit.,* p. 7.

7 *Ibid.,* p. 8.

8 Ormsby, *op. cit.,* p. 369.

9 Tien-Fang, Cheng, *Oriental Immigration in Canada* (Shanghai: The Commercial Press Ltd., 1931), p. 87.

10 *Statutes of British Columbia,* 1895, c. 20, s. 2.

11 *Statutes of Canada,* 1920, c. 46, s. 30.

12 Corbett, David C., *Canada's Immigration Policy* (Toronto: University of Toronto Press., 1957), p. 33.

13 Hawkins, Freda, *Canada and Immigration: Public Policy and Public Concern* (Montreal: McGill-Queen's University Press, 1972), p. 101. Reproduced by permission of the Minister of Supply and Services Canada.

14 Cited in Hawkins, *loc. cit.*

15 Brown, W. Norman, *The United States and India, Pakistan, Bangladesh* (Cambridge: Harvard University Press, 1972), p. 26.

16 *The Immigration Program 2, A Report of the Canadian Immigration and Population Study,* Manpower and Immigration (Ottawa: Information Canada, 1974), p. 110.

17 *Immigration '74, op. cit.,* p. 3.

18 *Ibid.,* p. 4.

19 Clairmont, D. H., and F. C. Wien, "Race Relations in Canada," *Sociological Focus,* 9:2, April 1976, p. 183.

20 Ferguson, *op. cit.,* p. 192.

21 Ashworth, Mary, *Immigrant Children and Canadian Schools,* (Toronto: McClelland and Stewart, 1975), p. 61.

22 Brown, *op. cit.,* p. 292.

23 Richmond, Anthony H., *Aspects of the Absorption and Adaptation of Immigrants,* Manpower and Immigration (Ottawa: Information Canada, 1974), p. 13.

24 *Ibid.,* p. 17.

25 Hawkins, *op. cit.,* p. 21.

26 Commission on International Development, *Partners in Development* (New York: Praeger Publishers, 1969), p. 79.

27 Anderson, George, "The Sweatshop Legacy: Still With Us in 1974," *The Labour Gazette,* 74:6, June 1974, p. 401.

28 *Ibid.,* p. 405.

29 *The Immigration Program 2, op. cit.,* p. 189.

Chapter 7

SOME EUROPEAN IMMIGRANTS

The five previous chapters concern themselves with visible minorities. Native Indians and Métis, Inuit, Blacks, Chinese and Japanese, and Other Asians all wear the badge of colour. Their difference from white Canadians is obvious and unalterable. In this chapter we briefly examine some relatively invisible minorities, European whites, of neither British nor French extraction. Italians, Ukrainians, and various sets of recent refugees are described separately. General observations are also made about the sort of reception that European entrants received before the 1920s and the way they are treated now. The chapter closes with some comparisons and contrasts between the experiences in Canada of these people and of the non-whites discussed earlier.

Italians

Italians have been in Canada for a long time. Perhaps the first Italian to set foot here was Giovanni Caboto, otherwise known as John Cabot, who discovered Newfoundland in 1497. By the mid-nineteenth century, Montreal contained more Italians than New York City. Many of the earliest arrivals were skilled, and some became owners and operators of hotels.[1] The building of the Canadian Pacific Railroad between 1880 and 1885 and other large projects of the time created a demand for labourers of all sorts. Italians helped fill the need. Indeed, construction became stereotyped as the Italian occupation.

The influx of Italians into Canada diminished after 1927 because the Italian Fascist Party, then in control of Italy, discouraged emigration and because the Canadian government restricted immigration during the economic depression of the 1930s. After World War II, however, immigration from Italy began on a truly large scale: whereas in 1941 only 18,703 persons of Italian ethnic background were living in Toronto, by 1961 the number had increased more than seven-fold. Of the latter, only 31.5 percent were Canadian-born.[2] According to the most recent ethnic census (1971), there are 730,820 persons of Italian background throughout the country, or about 3.4 percent of the total population.[3] Of these, 463,095 are in Ontario, 169,560 in Quebec, and 53,795 in British Columbia.[4]

Because of their relatively sizeable numbers and their concentration in fields like construction, earlier Italian immigrants often found it unnecessary to know English in order to obtain employment. The same was even more true of Italian women, who typically either remained at home or worked at low status jobs. Inability to use English caused many Italians to remain within their immediate community. At the same time, residence in segregated enclaves meant little opportunity to learn a new language.

The learning of English has remained a major task for recent Italian immigrants also. Most come from small villages and towns of southern Italy, or from Sicily and Sardinia—areas that are particularly poor, rural, and deficient in education. Few arrive with much proficiency as anglophones.

Some communities have been trying to make the language transition easier. For example, at the Saint Clare School and the Richard W. Scott School, both in Toronto, bilingual Italian-English classes are taught at the elementary school level by bilingual teachers. These classes are a joint experiment carried on by the Metropolitan Toronto Separate School Board and by the Ontario Institute for Studies in Education. Students in the programs are generally able to catch up to their native English-speaking peers, in about three years.[5]

Even so, in many Canadian cities Italian residential clustering remains conspicuous. In addition to the language barrier, reasons for this include the existence of special institutions including the parish church. The close-knit social structure found in these Italian communities helps their inhabitants have a voice in municipal affairs and in the labour movement.

Most Italian immigrants have little difficulty finding some employment. Traditionally strong bonds of kinship alleviate many of their readjustment problems. Indeed, 91 percent of all Italian immigrants are sponsored by close relatives, as compared to 47 percent for Canadian immigrants generally. In the mid-1950s, it was estimated that one Italian immigrant meant 49 sponsored relatives.[6] Moreover, new immigrants from Italy often work for relatives already settled in Canada. This tendency naturally contributes to a concentration of Italians within specific industries such as building construction, and that in turn has resulted in some of the new immigrants quickly attaining a relatively high standard of living. Strong labour unions in the building trades have also played a part in this process.

Some adjustments in work habits may be necessary, as people used to working haphazard hours on farms in southern Italy now have to conform to regular time schedules in industry. Conversely, Italians with professional competence but no working knowledge of English (or French) may be required to take jobs of lower status than those they had been accustomed to in their home country. In general, not only do Italian male immigrants work hard, but also about a third of their wives work outside the home.[7] Emphasis is placed on saving and personal sacrifice in order to buy property. For many Italian immigrants, material success has generated a fairly satisfied outlook, which tends both to reinforce the importance of the family unit and to foster a more generally conservative outlook.

Ukrainians

Early Ukrainian settlers in the nineteenth century were diverted to the prairie provinces. This region bore a strong resemblance to their Russian homeland: the soil was fertile and wheat was the major crop. In addition, many Ukrainians worked on railroad construction gangs. Mass immigration of Ukrainians occurred in three waves: between 1896 and 1914, in the 1920s, and after World War II. During the first wave, the Ukraine was an integral part of Tsarist Russia. Just prior to the second wave, it was an independent country. During the third, it was under Soviet domination. As of 1971, there were some 580,655 persons of Ukrainian background in Canada, or about 2.7 percent of the total population.[8] This figure includes 159,880 persons of Ukrainian background in Ontario and 114,410 in Manitoba. Winnipeg is clearly the centre of Ukrainian activities in this country. Most Ukrainian language publishing is located there. Despite their numbers and organization in Manitoba, however, no specifically Ukrainian provincial political party has ever been formed. Nor, given the Ukraine's present status as part of the USSR, can international support be reasonably sought after.

Up until 1916, Ukrainians in Manitoba were able to send their children to officially bilingual Ukrainian-English public schools; thereafter these schools were abolished. Saskatchewan and Alberta ended semi-official bilingual teaching in their public schools in 1919. These actions reflected some of the antagonisms and bitterness generated by World War I.

Since then, Ukrainians have striven to retain their language and culture through instruction outside the public school system. They have established student hostels at private schools and colleges, vernacular part-time schools in labour halls, parochial schools, summer schools, correspondence courses, and adult education programs. In addition, since World War II an estimated fifty established Ukrainian poets, writers, and scholars have settled in Canada, many of them continuing to publish in the Ukrainian language. The amount of poetry produced is particularly notable. The *Ukrainian Voice*, an ethnic newspaper published in Winnipeg, features many literary works by those immigrants.

The educational level of the Ukrainian population has been steadily moving upward, across generations. Though precise data are unavailable, many young Ukrainians are now enrolled in colleges and universities. Among more recent immigrants of Ukrainian background, about one in eight enters with secondary or university education already completed.

Concomitantly, after 1950 Ukrainians began shaking off their traditional status as agricultural or unskilled labourers. In 1941, about 55 percent of the Ukrainian male labour force was in agriculture, a figure that dropped to 35 percent by 1951 and to 23 percent by 1961.[9] Instead, they are moving into manufacturing or into clerical, managerial, and professional positions. Not surprisingly, seven out of ten Ukrainian immigrants now start their lives in Canada as urban, not rural, dwellers.

Refugees

Canada has long been considered a haven for victims of religious and political persecution. A few Jewish refugees from Hitler's Germany were admitted into the country during the 1930s. A large wave of so-called displaced persons, or D.P.s, arrived after 1947. These people had been uprooted from their central and east European homes as a result of World War II. Tens of thousands fleeing to the West from the Soviet Union were joined by others from the satellite countries. They were initially cared for in countries like Austria, France, and Britain. Most were later admitted into Canada, Australia, and the United States.

The government has two procedures for admitting special categories of persons. A Minister's Permit allows temporary entry of persons inadmissible under ordinary provisions of the law. Orders-in-Council, by contrast, provide special regulations superseding ordinary immigration rules in the cases to which they apply. In 1946, 4,527 former members of the Polish armed services were given entry under Order-in-Council, P.C. 3112. Between 1947 and 1952, a further 166,000 displaced persons were brought in under arrangements with the International Refugee Organization. These immigrants contracted to remain in a given occupation, usually agriculture, for at least one year.

In 1956, following the Hungarian uprising, the federal government launched preparations to admit Hungarian refugees. Sponsorship criteria were widened, medical examination procedures were relaxed, and free transportation by sea or air was provided. Some refugees were kept in France, Holland, and Britain until the spring of 1957, so that they might arrive in Canada after the usual winter employment slump. The entering Hungarians included college students and instructors. Indeed, the entire forestry faculty of Hungary's University of Sopron moved to the University of British Columbia. By October 1957, about thirty-six thousand Hungarian refugees had entered the country.[10] The total cost of the program amounted to fifteen million dollars.

A third large group of refugees was admitted during the World Refugee Year of 1960. Through reduced admission requirements, some thirty-five hundred were allowed in between July 1, 1959 and June 30, 1960. (By the end of 1960, the post-World War II total of refugees entering Canada rose to 238,539.)[11] Special emphasis during 1960 was also placed on the admission of handicapped immigrants sponsored by individuals and voluntary organizations.

A fourth major refugee movement occurred between September 1968 and March 1969, when 11,153 Czechoslovakian refugees were admitted following the Soviet invasion of their country. Again, normal requirements were temporarily relaxed. Considerable assistance was provided the refugees after arrival, with the cost of the program totalling about nine million dollars. [12]

Beginning with the Hungarians of 1956, the federal government adopted a vigorous policy of planning and managing the placement of refugees. The intent was that they be distributed fairly evenly across the country, rather than becoming concentrated in one urban centre. Under the Air Bridge to Canada Program, special charter flights were arranged, with a flat fare of two hundred dollars per adult and one hundred dollars per child, regardless of their destination. Some 17,565 refugees used the Air Bridge; of 207 flights, all but 78 terminated in western provinces. [13]

Official Canadian concern for refugees is also reflected in its participation within, and contributions to, the Office of the United Nations High Commissioner for Refugees and (between 1957 and 1962) the Intergovernmental Committee for European Migration. Compared with most other nations of the world, Canada's overall record in settling refugees and other displaced persons is commendable. [14] The country is willing to pay its international humanitarian dues, also. In 1973, it contributed $450,000 to the High Commissioner for Refugees. And this does not include the donations to special refugee programs in East Pakistan, the Sudan, and Bangladesh, the latter alone receiving $13,200,000 in 1972 and $8,592,000 in 1973. [15]

Early Problems

One should not imagine that the transition to life in Canada was easy for European immigrants. At one time, they were considered not only a cheap source of labour but also expendable. Twenty-three percent of all industrial accidents in Canada between 1904 and 1911 occurred in railroad construction, where most immigrant workers were employed and where little attempt was made to enforce safety regulations. [16] Immigrants were always assigned the most difficult and hazardous jobs in the mining industry. As one mine operator put it, "Canadians won't work in the mines. They are quite willing to boss the job but they are not going to do the rough work themselves . . . What we want is brawn and muscle, and we get it." [17] Moreover, if immigrant workers went out on strike for better wages or conditions, the stoppage was likely to be broken up by police or troops. W. A. Woods, president of Vallance Coal Company, for example, urged Prime Minister Borden to send troops into mining areas "to make the foreigners work at the point of a bayonet." [18]

During World War I, some European ethnic groups were victims of war hysteria. In the war's earlier stage (1914-1916), press and Parliament often raised questions about whether aliens from enemy countries should be allowed to hold jobs while Anglo-Canadians went unemployed. Allusions to possible security risks and subversion were also common. By 1917, however, Canada was experiencing manpower shortages. Then the questions began to change. Should aliens from enemy countries be permitted to refuse work? Should they not instead be forced to work?

The Russian Revolution, which brought the Bolsheviks into power, occurred in 1917. The threat of Bolshevism made constant headlines and many wondered whether Russian aliens ought to be deported. Foreign language presses were often suppressed and socialist or anarchist organizations outlawed. The Ukrainian Socialist Democrat Party was just one victim of the suppression.[19] Severe fines and penalties fell upon groups failing to comply with government directives. In addition, those Ukrainians who had not yet become citizens saw further naturalizations suspended in 1918, ostensibly because they were aliens from a former enemy country.[20]

Another problem facing immigrants in 1919 arose from the need to find jobs for demobilized members of the Canadian armed forces. Mining and lumber companies laid off thousands of aliens in order to provide openings. The International Nickel Company, for example, dismissed twenty-two hundred of its thirty-two hundred employees, most of them immigrants. As a result, many Germans and Ukrainians returned voluntarily to Europe.

Sometimes the hostility took a more vicious turn. In January 1919 a band of ex-servicemen attacked scores of Ukrainians, and in particular destroyed the business operated by Sam Blumenberg, a prominent Socialist in Manitoba. Police, militia, and the RCMP all refused to intervene.[21] Anglo-Canadian vigilante groups soon sprang up: these included the Citizens' Committee of One Thousand and the Defenders of the Canadian Way of Life in Winnipeg. Such groups were often influential in provincial government, and they had much of the business community on their side. As the President of the Canadian Manufacturers' Association stated in 1919:

> Canada should not encourage the immigration of those whose political and social beliefs unfit them for assimilation with Canadians. While a great country such as Canada possessing millions of vacant acres needs population, it is wiser to go slowly and secure the right sort of citizens.[22]

Recent Trends

One should not draw too sharp a contrast between Canadian's receptivity toward immigrants before World War I and after World War II, or paint recent conditions in unrelievedly cheery tones. For example, according to a study of the construction industry in 1961-62, "the part played by discrimination and exploitation cannot be overlooked." Immigrant workers were receiving 85 cents to $1.50 an hour, compared to the usual nationwide average of $1.94. Sometimes employers failed to pay for overtime or legal holiday. On occasion, worthless paycheques were issued or kickbacks demanded from workers. Mandatory contributions for workmen's compensation and unemployment insurance might also be skipped, with the result that some immigrants were disqualified from receiving benefits they deserved. [23]

Exploitation of female immigrants was also common. In the province of Quebec, for example, Italian women working in certain branches of the textile industry received extremely low pay for long hours of work. [24]

More blatant indicators of hostility toward immigrants during and after World War II can readily be found as well. While the war was going on, the Ukrainian-Labour-Farmer Temples were declared illegal and their 108 halls placed under the Custodian of Enemy Alien Property. By the time the ban was lifted, sixteen of the halls had already been sold. [25] Under the War Measures Act, moreover, several hundred persons of Italian background were detained. In Montreal, for example, "almost overnight, the RCMP wiped out the leadership of the Italian community by sending virtually all the leaders to the internment camp at Petawawa." [26] Within weeks, though, almost all were released. Discrimination against Italian immigrants in Montreal was also intense between 1948 and 1955, when gangs of French youth would go looking on the streets for *"les maudits Italiens"* to beat up. [27]

At present, the preferences that Italians and other European immigrants demonstrate for school instruction in the English language is again creating stress in Quebec. On the one hand, there are the habitual practices of the immigrants:

> Nearly all Roman Catholic immigrants in Quebec have sent their children to English rather than French schools. In Montreal in 1962-63, for example, 92 per cent of those of Ukrainian origin who were in Catholic schools were in English rather than French schools. The figures for other cultural groups are almost as high: 88 per cent of Poles, 84 per cent of Portuguese, 83 per cent of Germans, 80 per cent of Hungarians, 77 per cent of Spanish, and 75 per cent of Italians. [28]

On the other hand, there is Quebec's long-standing concern over the continued vitality of the French language, as expressed, for example, in a statement from the Office of the Minister of Education and Cultural Affairs in 1973:

> With Quebec's decreasing birth rate, immigration is fast becoming the stabilizing factor between the two linguistic groups. Most New Canadian children are enrolling in English schools. This trend can completely upset Quebec's linguistic structure in the not too distant future unless positive action is taken to promote the enrollment of immigrant children in French schools. . . .

Department of Education statistics for the 1971-72 school year reveal that, in public schools, out of a total of 65,105 children whose mother tongue was neither French nor English, 55,490 were being taught in English; and 9,270 in French. . . .

Up to now, French schools have not displayed any great spirit of hospitality towards immigrant children. To ward off foreign influence, these institutions have traditionally erected cultural, social and religious barriers that have contributed to set these children apart. Not only have they made no arrangements to foster integration of these children, but they have sometimes forced upon them a religious teaching at variance with their beliefs and have only reluctantly admitted the presence of representatives of other ethnic groups.[29]

The response of the Quebec legislature was to pass a bill in 1974 directing that all immigrant children in the province must attend French language schools unless they could prove they were proficient in English.[30] Since then, additional legal and administrative steps have been taken to bring this policy into effect.

Overall, acceptance of immigrants in Canada is still inhibited by a prejudiced and injurious stereotyping rife throughout the country. True, Canadians are willing to accept refugees from countries undergoing political turmoil, provided their own stability is not jeopardized.[31] But their usual view of immigrants as poor, starved, pathetic creatures, grateful for the chance merely to enter Canada, does not reflect postwar reality. Ignorance accounts for much of the misconception. As the Ontario Economic Council noted in 1970:

The public is generally apathetic. Many Canadians have no conception of the size of the new population, have never entertained an immigrant in their home nor carried on a personal conversation with one. Like some immigrant groups, they live in their own 'closed' communities. They read newspaper and magazine articles which depict the gaiety and happiness of the lives of new Canadians and relate their success stories. They tend to believe that all immigrants are doing extremely well in the new country and are very fortunate to be here. . . .[32]

This lack of correct, first-hand information helps explain why public images of immigrants have remained relatively unchanged, despite substantial shifts of late in the character of immigration. In Hawkin's words:

The image has been a lower-class one inherited from the great migrations of the nineteenth and early twentieth centuries. The army of migrating engineers, doctors, scientists, graduate nurses, and secretaries has not yet quite obliterated the mental picture of the poor, huddled immigrant family with its meagre possessions and hungry look.[33]

Other more specific misconceptions about immigrants occur. Often they are blamed for the problems of the cities. Their increasing numbers are held to exacerbate housing shortages, elevate crime rates, bring on infectious diseases, overwhelm welfare and other governmental services, and cause unemployment among Canadian citizens. The problems are real enough. But according to the 1975 Report of the Special Joint Committee on Immigration Policy of the Senate and the House of Commons, they stem primarily from more general economic, social, and cultural conditions in the cities themselves. It is internal movement, from rural to urban areas and among the provinces, that provides the main impulse for city growth.

> Immigrants are only a tributary flowing into a much larger river of Canadians who have been migrating to the cities in ever increasing numbers throughout the century. This does not mean that the Committee is not sympathetic to the planning needs of cities. It simply feels that immigrants should not be blamed for problems that they have done little to cause, although they may have compounded them. Canadians worried about the quality of life in our cities should look elsewhere than to sharply reduced immigration for a solution to the problems of city living.[34]

In addition, newcomers to Canada do not take more advantage of governmental social services, health care, and other benefits than do native-born Canadians. On the contrary, their use of them falls below the national average, if only because such assistance is traditionally provided by the family in their home countries. Nor do immigrants contribute disproportionately to the crime rate. According to Professor Frederick Zemans of Osgood Hall, ". . . most immigrants who come to Canada have a strong fear of the legal system itself . . . and they are very concerned that they should not get into any difficulties or any trouble while in this country." Indeed, a study prepared for the Solicitor General in 1974 indicated that the crime rate of immigrants was approximately half that of native-born Canadians.[35]

Of late, industrial and trade unions have improved immigrants' working conditions. Organizing these workers in the first place, though, is far from easy. Employers sometimes oppose these efforts strenuously and overtly.[36] Workers, too, may be hard to communicate with—due to an inability to speak French or English—or unaware of their rights or fearful of losing their jobs. Outside organizers may find themselves frustrated by a hastily interposed company union dominated by the employer, or by actual plant closings. Knowing all this, unions are sometimes reluctant to begin the organizing process among immigrant workers.

Provincial minimum wage laws provide some legal protection. Yet the enforcement machinery is often weak. Quebec's Minimum Wage Act provides for a Minimum Wage Commission, but that Commission goes into action only after a complaint has been registered. Montreal is allotted just fifty inspectors to visit its business firms and plants. Besides, fines of ten to one hundred dollars are no deterrent to unscrupulous employers. Complaints have led to investigations revealing dishwashers working a 66-hour week for fifty dollars, pieceworker sewing machine operators labouring 135 hours in a given week with no overtime pay, and other payments of straight time where overtime was appropriate.[37]

Nowadays all major European immigrant groups have their own social institutions, clubs, fraternal societies, and churches. Citizenship classes and English or French language classes are available to them, and many attend such courses. Governmental authorities emphasize integration, however, rather than assimilation or Canadianization. They do not consider the partial segregation of immigrants to be undesirable. This policy meets with the approval of most ethnic groups.

Comparisons and Contrasts

In general, Europeans coming to Canada have experienced fewer hostilities or disabilities than have native and coloured immigrant populations. They have not been pushed onto reserves or expected to live off frozen lands. No exclusionary laws have been drawn up against them or gentlemen's agreements concluded with their home governments. Nor has anyone questioned their ability to survive the climate.

With minor exceptions, such as the so-called "enemy aliens" during and just after World War I, European immigrants have habitually been able to seek naturalization.[38] And once having become citizens, they enjoy all the legal rights and privileges accruing to native-born English or French Canadians. They have neither been denied the franchise from the start nor had it taken away. Vote prohibitions have not been imposed on them at the provincial level and then elevated to the federal level. Veteran's organizations have not had to plead that an exception be made for Europeans who fought in World War I, so that they at least could participate in the electoral process.

European immigrants have not been forced into segregated schools, except as local concentration may induce an ethnically homogeneous student body. If they opted for parochial schooling, they did so voluntarily; it was not a case of the churches' having had to fill a governmental void. Besides, many of the more recent immigrants enter Canada with most or all of their education completed.

Europeans, to be sure, have not invariably received equal treatment in the labour market. Like other newcomers, they have sometimes been taken advantage of—paid less than was their right, exposed to inadequate safety precautions, kept from joining unions. As last hired, they were often first fired—and that from jobs in lower-rung industries. But at least they have not been confined to unskilled work, or exhibited sky-high unemployment rates, or been denied entry into various job markets by law, or denied licences because they were excluded from voters' rolls, or been kept at an artificially low pay scale so that their will to return to the land would not be dulled.

Europeans have enjoyed the legal freedom to live wherever they could afford, though in practice their tendency to reside in their own ethnically segregated neighbourhoods was not entirely self-imposed. Poorly enforced human rights legislation, after all, is no deterrent to the landlord who refuses to rent to certain minorities. Even so, few restrictive covenants have been drawn up against Europeans as they have against those whose skin is of a different hue. Europeans have not been confined to rural shanty towns. They have rarely been forced into internment camps and seen their properties sold over their protests at deflated prices.

Although new European immigrants still experience initial unemployment or underemployment, this is only to be expected, given their unfamiliarity with the Canadian labour market, their problems with the language, and the fact that their credentials may lack domestic acceptance. But within a very few years they achieve parity with native-born Canadians. Certainly, most postwar European immigrants have soon enjoyed the prevailing standard of living. It is length of residence and level of income, not racial background, that primarily accounts for the degree of their success here.

European immigrants, some claim, are strongly determined to better themselves. They have known harsh conditions in their homeland; for them Canada is a land of opportunity. Yet it is obvious that such opportunity has not always been fairly or equally distributed. If some native and immigrant groups do not seem to try enough, may it not be that in the past, and even now, there has been too little for them to try for? It may well take a generation or more of educational improvement, long-term job experience, better housing, and other material satisfactions before the viability of a new and a more just social reality can be fully established.

NOTES

[1] Spada, A. V., *The Italians in Canada* (Montreal: Riviera Printers, 1969), p. 52.

[2] Jansen, Clifford J., "The Italian Community in Toronto," in Elliot Jean L., *Minority Canadians 2, Immigrant Groups* (Scarborough: Prentice-Hall of Canada, 1971), p. 208.

[3] *Special Bulletin 1971 Census of Canada, Population, Specified Ethnic Groups*, Statistics Canada (Ottawa: Information Canada, 1974), p. 61.

[4] *Ibid.*, p. 1.

[5] Ashworth, Mary, *Immigrant Children and Canadian Schools* (Toronto: McClelland and Stewart, 1975), p. 56. Reprinted with permission of the Minister of Supply and Services Canada.

[6] Hawkins, Freda, *Canada and Immigration: Public Policy and Public Concern* (Montreal: McGill-Queen's University Press, 1972), p. 51.

[7] Boissevain, Jeremy, *The Italians of Montreal: Social Adjustment in a Plural Society*, Studies of the Royal Commission on Bilingualism and Biculturalism (Ottawa: Information Canada, 1974), p. 16.

[8] *Special Bulletin 1971 Census of Canada, op. cit.*, p. 1.

[9] Isajiw, Wsevolod, and Norbert J. Hartmann, 1970, "Changes in the occupational structure of Ukrainians in Canada: a methodology for the study of changes in ethnic status,"

in *Social and Cultural Change in Canada.* Vol. I, W. E. Mann ed., (Vancouver: Copp Clark, 1970), pp. 100-01.

[10] Richmond, Anthony H., *Post-War Immigrants in Canada* (Toronto: University of Toronto Press, 1967), p. 14.

[11] *Ibid.*, p. 15.

[12] Hawkins, *op. cit.*, p. 407.

[13] *Ibid.*, pp. 116 and 406.

[14] In 1975, some 4,030 refugees were admitted from South Vietnam and Cambodia, and 3,930 from Chile. See Freda Hawkins, "Destination Unknown: Difficult Decisions on Immigration Policy," *Queen's Quarterly*, 82:4, Winter 1975, p. 593. For the Chilean refugees also see *The Immigration Program 2*, A Report of the Canadian Immigration and Population Study, Manpower and Immigration (Ottawa: Information Canada, 1974), p. 112.

[15] *Immigration and Population Statistics*, Manpower and Immigration (Ottawa: Information Canada, 1974), p. 111.

[16] Avery, Donald, "Continental European Immigrant Workers in Canada, 1896-1919: From 'Stalwart Peasants' to Radical Proletariat," *Canadian Review of Sociology and Anthropology*, 12:1, February 1975, p. 56.

[17] Cited in Avery, *op. cit.*, p. 57.

[18] Cited in Avery, *op. cit.*, p. 58.

[19] *Ibid.*, p. 61.

[20] The Ukraine was part of Russia and Russia, under Lenin, had come to an understanding with Germany in the Treaty of Brest-Litovsk. At that time (1917-20) there was also an independent Ukrainian Republic.

[21] Avery, *op. cit.*, p. 63.

[22] Cited in Avery, *op. cit.*, p. 64.

[23] *Report of the Royal Commission on Labour Management Relations in the Construction Industry* (H. C. Goldenberg, Commissioner). (Ottawa: Ontario Provincial Executive Council Office, March 1962).

[24] Drea, Frank, "Lucia's Trying Love Affair with Canada," *Chatelaine*, April 1960, p. 11.

[25] Marx, Herbert, "The Emergency Power and Civil Liberties in Canada," *McGill Law Journal*, 16:1, March 1970, p. 78.

[26] Boissevain, *op. cit.*, p. 7.

[27] *Ibid.*, p. 59.

[28] *Report of the Royal Commission on Bilingualism and Biculturalism*, cited in Ashworth, *op. cit.*, p. 14.

[29] Cited in Ashworth, *op. cit.*, p. 15.

[30] *Ibid.*, p. 16.

[31] Tienhaara, Nancy, *Canadian Views on Immigration and Population: An Analysis of Post-War Gallup Polls* (Ottawa: Information Canada, 1974), p.4. Reproduced by permission of the Minister of Supply and Services Canada.

[32] Cited in Tienhaara, *op. cit.*, p. 44.

[33] Hawkins, *op. cit.*, p. 30.

[34] *Report to Parliament by the Special Joint Committee on Immigration Policy*, (Ottawa: Information Canada, 1975), p. 8. Reproduced by permission of the Minister of Supply and Services Canada.

[35] *Ibid.*, pp. 9-10.

[36] Drea, *op. cit.*, p. 11.

[37] *The Labour Gazette*, 74:6, June 1974, p. 410.

[38] Other exceptions include the Hutterites and Doukhobors, both to be discussed in our second volume.

Chapter 8
AN OVERVIEW

This final chapter provides tabular summaries of various issues discussed throughout the book. Properly constructed, synoptic tables enhance comprehension by simplifying and streamlining material. Their purpose is to reduce, rather than increase, confusion.

Of the tables presented, the first two furnish population data on particular minorities, for Canada as a whole and for individual provinces.[1] Information is presented in both absolute and percentage terms. Of the next three tables, one concerns restrictions that were, at some time or other, lawfully imposed on at least one of the minorities. The other two examine attributes of the minorities, or of the social system surrounding them, that might help explain the relative severity of these impositions. The last table focuses on recent immigrants and, using housing conditions as an indicator, asks to what degree under today's more enlightened and prosperous conditions minority newcomers approach or fall short of normal Canadian living standards.

Small Populations and the Democratic Calculus

Table 1 specifies population sizes, according to the 1971 census, that relate to the most groups described in the preceding chapters.[2] (Figures have been rounded off to the nearest thousand.) Classifications used in the census are generally consistent with those employed in our narratives: thus, "Italian," "Ukrainian," "Canadian Indian," "Chinese and Japanese," and "Inuit." In addition, "East Indian," "Pakistani," and "Other East Asian" more or less correspond to our "Other Asians," while the designation "Negro and West Indian" is a reasonably close approximation of "Blacks."[3]

All together, these ethnic groups total nearly two million people. But of that number, fully two out of three are either Italians or Ukrainians, minority Europeans who were introduced into the narrative, in part at least, to provide a contrasting background. The non-Europeans in Table 1, both natives and immigrants, total just under six hundred thousand.

According to the 1971 census, Ontario is home to far more minority Canadians than any other province. Its eight hundred and ten thousand figure is more than half a million higher than any other, and by itself exceeds 40 percent of the Canadian total. Ontario has the most Italians, most Ukrainians, most Canadian Indians, most Other Asians, most

Table 1
Ethnic Group Populations by Province, 1971
(in thousands)

	All Canada	Newfound-land	PEI	Nova Scotia	New Brunswick	Quebec	Ontario	Manitoba	Saskatchewan	Alberta	British Columbia	Yukon	NWT
Italian	731	—	—	4	1	170	463	10	3	25	54	—	—
Ukrainian	581	—	—	2	1	20	160	114	86	136	60	1	1
Canadian Indian	295	1	—	4	4	33	62	43	40	45	52	3	7
Chinese and Japanese	156	1	—	1	1	14	55	5	5	17	58	—	—
Other Asian: East Indian Pakistani and Other East Asian	68	—	—	1	—	7	31	3	2	4	19	—	—
Black: Negro and West Indian	62	—	—	6	1	10	38	2	1	2	2	—	—
Inuit	18	1	—	—	—	4	1	—	—	—	—	—	11
Sum*	1,911	4	1	19	8	257	810	178	137	229	245	4	20

*Sums may differ slightly from column totals because of rounding.
N.B. A dash means less than .5 thousand.
Source: Aggregated and rounded off from data in *Population Specified Ethnic Groups*, Statistics Canada, May 1974 (Ottawa: Information Canada, 1974).

Table 2
Ethnic Group Populations by Province, 1971
(in percentages)

	All Canada	Newfoundland	PEI	Nova Scotia	New Brunswick	Quebec	Ontario	Manitoba	Saskatchewan	Alberta	British Columbia	Yukon	NWT
Italian	3	—	—	—	—	3	6	1	—	2	2	1	1
Ukrainian	3	—	—	—	—	—	2	12	10	8	3	3	2
Canadian Indian	1	—	—	1	—	1	1	4	4	3	2	14	21
Chinese and Japanese	1	—	—	—	—	—	1	—	1	1	3	1	—
Other Asian: East Indian	1						1			1	2		
Pakistani and Other East Asian													
Black: Negro and West Indian	—			1									
Inuit	—												33
All minorities listed above*	9	1	1	3	1	4	11	18	15	14	12	22	57
All non-white minorities listed above*	3	1	1	2	1	1	3	6	5	4	7	17	54

*Sums may differ slightly from column totals because of rounding.

N.B. A dash means less than 0.5 percent.

Source: Aggregated and rounded off from data in *Population Specified Ethnic Groups*, Statistics Canada, May 1974 (Ottawa: Information Canada, 1974).

Blacks. Only for the combined Chinese and Japanese, where British Columbia was barely leading, and for the Inuit, is Ontario not in front. Ontario is the province of ethnic minorities *par excellence;* Toronto's magnetism for immigrants seems likely to sustain that pre-eminence.

Of the remaining provinces, British Columbia comes third, just after Quebec. British Columbia is first or second on three of the non-white groups (Chinese and Japanese conjointly, Canadian Indians, and Other Asians), while Quebec, whose total is largely explained by its Italian component, is second on two others (Blacks and Inuit). Prairie province figures mainly reflect Ukrainian immigration, though Canadian Indians contribute sizeably as well. Among the Atlantic provinces, only Nova Scotia has a noteworthy and diversified population of minority ethnics. However, even if one adds to it the figures for New Brunswick, Newfoundland, and Prince Edward Island, the sum, approximately thirty-three thousand, is far less than that for any other subdivision except the Yukon and Northwest Territories.

Examination of raw population figures, whether singly or in tandem, can carry one just so far. Inhibiting the analysis is the fact that provinces vary widely in total number of residents, from Ontario with more than 7.7 million in 1971 to the Yukon with less than 19,000. To assess the impact of ethnic minorities on Canada and its provinces, it is necessary to take some account of these varying sizes. The easiest way to do so is to convert the absolute numbers of Table 1 into the percentages of Table 2. [4]

The seven ethnic categories in Table 2 account for one Canadian in eleven. Only in the Northwest Territories do they—principally Inuit and Canadian Indians—form a majority. Elsewhere, they vary from a high of 18 percent in Manitoba to a low of just one percent in three of the four Atlantic provinces.

If one omits the two European minorities, however, and concentrates only on the five non-white groups, the percentages decrease dramatically. The overall Canadian total then stands at just 3 percent. Results for each prairie province diminish by at least 10 percent, largely because Ukrainians form so large a category there. Ontario shows itself to be just about at the 1971 national average, its large lead in Table 1 traceable both to its general size and to Quebec's falling so far short of the norm. Canadian Indians, Inuit, Blacks, Chinese and Japanese, and Other Asians, separately and together, contribute insignificant percentages to the Atlantic provinces, even when the small sizes of those political units are taken into account. While these minorities are met a bit more frequently in the West, only in the North (principally through the presence of native peoples) do they form a large element in the population.

It is obvious that the democratic vote process generally cannot work to the direct advantage of these ethnic groups. Only the Ukrainians in Manitoba and Saskatchewan, the Canadian Indians in the Yukon and

Northwest Territories, and the Inuit in the Northwest Territories constituted more than 10 percent of a given province's population, thereby
provincially exceeding the minority standard established in Chapter 1. If
the cutting line is lowered to 5 percent, this adds only the Italians in Ontario and the Ukrainians in Alberta. Conversely, of the eighty-four pro-
vincial-minority cells in Table 2, all but twenty contain percentages
below 2.[5]

The true potential for influence through the ballot box is even slighter
than these figures suggest. After all, despite our aggregating them,
Chinese are not Japanese, nor are new immigrants necessarily similar to
older residents of the same ethnic origin. The Other Asian category is
heterogeneous in the extreme. The Black populace is exceedingly diverse. And Canadian Indians are reft by all kinds of cleavages. These
and other minorities scarcely vote as blocks, and they lack organization
and leaders that can credibly speak on behalf of the group as a whole.

Moreover, despite efforts by all major political parties to recruit at
least some ethnic candidates in ethnic ridings, the impact of the native
and immigrant non-white community remains relatively weak, particularly at the federal level. Multicultural policy is just beginning to get
political attention, given the emphasis on Canada as a bilingual and bicultural (French-English) nation. Indeed, so long as white Canadians
feel threatened by the increasing diversion of the country's population,
participation of minorities in the political process will probably not advance much.

The likeliest solution to all this lies in a greater humanitarian maturity
and understanding among senior elected and appointed officials of
government, reflective of Canada's growing role in a multi-coloured international world,[6] in the translation of that maturity into policies and
programs at both federal and provincial levels, and in the gradual per-
meation of these newer values of acceptance and fostering among the
general populace. Only then can the democratic calculus usefully re-
emerge as people in general across the country, expressing their better
selves rather than their immediate interests, validate what benefits the
entire social system and not just their particular corner of it.

Past Restrictions

Democratic procedures surely did little to prevent restrictions from
being imposed on non-European minorities in the past. Even if one
limits the survey to the period since Confederation, a full dozen restrictive categories can be specified, as indicated in Table 3. These include
the areas of employment, housing, public accommodations, voting,
medical and social welfare, land purchase, immigration, education, citizenship, arbitrary search and seizure, use of liquor, and taxation. Discrimination in more than half these areas befell every single non-white
minority analyzed here.

Table 3

Restrictions Imposed on Minorities

	Chinese and Japanese	Other Asians	Canadian Indians	Inuit	Blacks	European Immigrants	All
Employment	x	x	x	x	x	x	6
Housing	x	x	x	x	x	x	6
Public Accommodations	x	x	x	x	x		5
Voting	x	x	x	x			4
Medical and Social Welfare	x		x	x	x		4
Immigration	x	x			x	x	4
Citizenship	x	x	x			x	4
Arbitrary Search and Seizure	x	x	x			x	4
Land Purchase	x	x			x		3
Education			x	x	x		3
Use of Liquor			x	x			2
Taxation	x	x					2
All	10	9	9	7	7	5	47

N.B. An "x" in a box denotes the existence at some time of a particular restriction on a minority, the restriction being defined by the row, and the minority by the column, whose intersection forms that box. Blank boxes indicate the absence of such minority restrictions.

Were it not that restrictions on land purchase and immigration possessed little or no relevance for native peoples, Canadian Indians would lead the list of those suffering. As it is, they are tied with Other Asians and rank just below the Chinese and Japanese, who escaped discriminatory treatment only in education and use of liquor. Inuit and Blacks fared somewhat better, never having been subjected to special taxes, arbitrary search and seizure, or revocation of citizenship. Blacks were also the sole non-European minority that always retained eligibility to vote.

The slowly descending trend line from Chinese and Japanese through Inuit, which moves from ten restrictive topics to seven, drops even further as European immigrants (i.e., Italians and Ukrainians) are considered. Although they experienced frequent instances of discrimination in employment and housing and some may argue that they did suffer briefly during wartime from some arbitrary (if legal) searches and seizures as well as from some minor delays in immigration and citizenship, Italians and Ukrainians were always legally entitled to utilize public accommodations, participate in voting, enjoy medical and social welfare schemes, purchase land, and benefit from public education.[7]

Variations in the incidence of discrimination can in principle be reasonably traced either to inveterate characteristics of the minorities or to attributes of the encompassing social situation or to both. Table 4 lists five general ways in which ethnic groups may depart from the Anglo-French mainstream. These are: race, language, culture, religion, and recency of arrival. During their first major generation of residence in Canada, when the reactions of their English and French neighbours would have been largely set, all but the European immigrants were different in race, while only Blacks from the beginning had no problems with the English language, other than those of dialect and idiom.[8] Except for the Blacks and Europeans, all the minorities emerged from cultural backgrounds that deviated very sharply from the bicultural norm. Finally, native peoples have, of course, been here from the beginning and ancestors of many Blacks nearly so; in comparison the rest are relative (i.e., post-Confederation) newcomers. At the beginning, too, only Blacks and European immigrants normally professed some form of Christianity.

To facilitate inspection, the columns of Table 4 (and 5) are arranged in the same order as those in Table 3. Were the five characteristics cumulatively to explain differences in the impact of discrimination, column totals in 4 would fall off as one moves from left to right. And this is in fact largely the case. Chinese, Japanese, and Other Asians are "wrong" on all five variables, and they have suffered more variously. European immigrants, by contrast, have only language peculiarities and recency of arrival isolating them, and they have met fewer restrictions. The only group seriously out of place in Table 4 is the Blacks, who though deviant only in race have experienced prejudice in at least seven respects.

Another interpretation looks to the spread of hostility in the sur-

Table 4
Noticeable Characteristics of Minorities

	Chinese and Japanese	Other Asians	Canadian Indians	Inuit	Blacks	European Immigrants	All
Race	x	x	x	x	x		5
Language	x	x	x	x		x	5
Culture	x	x	x	x			4
Religion	x	x	x	x			4
Recent Arrival	x	x				x	3
All	5	5	4	4	1	2	21

N.B. An "x" indicates that the first sizeable Canadian generation of the minority in that row differed on the variable in that column from the English/French norms.

Table 5
Sources of Opposition to Minorities

	Chinese and Japanese	Other Asians	Canadian Indians	Inuit	Blacks	European Immigrants	All
Organized Labour	x	x	x	x	x	x	6
Citizens' Associations	x	x	x		x	x	5
Political Parties	x	x	x		x	x	5
War Veterans	x	x			x		3
Farm Organizations	x	x					2
Merchants		x	x				2
All	5	6	4	1	4	3	23

N.B. An "x" denotes at least one important, well-documented act of opposition by the category in that row toward the minority in that column. Blank boxes indicate the absence of such documentation.

rounding environment. Sources of opposition have been classified in Table 5 under six headings: organized labour, citizens' associations, political parties, war veterans, farm organizations, and merchants. Xenophobia was particularly common within labour circles, demonstrating once again that economic liberalism and civil libertarianism need not go hand in hand.[9] Not surprisingly, ethnic antagonisms have also been expressed frequently by citizens' associations; indeed, many of them were *ad hoc* groups formed for just that purpose. Established political parties also tend to express the prejudices of locally dominant majorities and if they do not, new parties may arise. The remaining analytical categories each opposed no more than half the ethnic minorities discussed here.

Once again, column totals fall off as one moves from left to right. All six groupings in the greater society often opposed Other Asians, and most opposed the Chinese and Japanese as well. Canadian Indians and Blacks (the latter more sporadically) have attracted a variety of opponents. Yet this array, too, does not fully account for the distribution of restrictions. In particular, hardly anyone disliked the Inuit, but they still suffered in manifold ways. They were out of sight and therefore out of mind. Until recently unnoticed and forgotten, they were victims of non-feasance rather than of mal-feasance.

Taken together, Tables 3 through 5 paint a gloomy historical picture. Non-white minorities have suffered from various discriminatory treatment. White minorities have suffered, too, though in fewer ways. Sometimes the experience accorded with laws on the books; sometimes it merely reflected common practice (though practice that courts would usually uphold). In general, the more ways ethnic groups departed from the bicultural norm and the more kinds of organized hostility they attracted from the surrounding community, the greater the range of disabilities that were imposed. Yet even a relatively conforming group, like the Blacks, or one with little overt opposition, like the Inuit, could suffer massively from accepted practice or isolation.

New Conditions

From a legal perspective at least, things are generally much better now. Discriminatory legislation has been wiped off the books. Citizens are not denied the vote because of ethnic background. A Canadian Bill of Rights has existed at the federal level since 1960. The years since World War II have also seen Human Rights Codes, Equal Pay Acts, Fair Employment Practices Acts, and Fair Accommodation Practices Acts enacted in most provinces. Many of these statutes make provision for some sort of official human rights agency to monitor their application and to negotiate, or force, fuller compliance.[10]

Still, the millenium has not yet arrived. Without eternal vigilance, progress may cease and conditions worsen. Recent developments in the Far North may even mean that peoples formerly left alone become the potential prey of private and governmental developers. Consider again, for example, the Province of Quebec's tactics in the James Bay Development Project.[11]

When Quebec initiated that twelve billion dollar hydroelectric enterprise, it refused to negotiate at all with the Crees and Inuit living in the areas. The natives went to court in November 1973, seeking (and obtaining) an injunction to stop the work. And a two-year legal battle followed.

In order to settle out of court, Quebec offered $63,000 to the Indians. This was rejected. Later, an agreement was negotiated between, on the one hand, the Grand Council of the Crees, representing individual bands at Fort George and other northern Quebec communities, and the Northern Quebec Inuit Association, representing fifteen Inuit communities; and, on the other hand, the government of Quebec, the James Bay

Energy Corporation, the James Bay Development Corporation, Hydro-Quebec, and the federal government of Canada. The native people agreed to stop litigation and permit development of the power complex in the valley of the LaGrande River. They also gave up all rights they might otherwise have to 410,000 square miles of territory, or about two-thirds the area of Quebec. In return, they were guaranteed payments of $225,000,000 spread over the next twenty years. Their rights of exclusive hunting, fishing, and trapping in certain areas were validated. They were given considerable self-government, a voice in all decisions affecting the local environment, and an opportunity to participate as investors and paid workers in future developments in the area. A James Bay Native Development Corporation would also oversee the creation of new industries for the Cree.

Now, this story may seem too good to be true. After being offered nothing and then virtually nothing, the Crees and Inuit receive nearly a quarter of a billion dollars. And since there are only about ten thousand natives in the area, this means $22,500 for every man, woman, and child. But from other viewpoints, the settlement is not overly generous. Indian and Inuit land claims have been extinguished at a cost of $225,000,000 for an area that contains an estimated $26,000,000,000 in copper and zinc alone—or less than a penny for every dollar of those two ores. Per year, the payment works out to only $1,125 for each native individual or $5,625 for a family of five. Such sums reduce the government's need to make welfare payments to these natives, and since much of the money is to be ploughed back into native development of industries, the government is also relieved of certain investment costs it might otherwise have had to shoulder.

New immigrants do not find all streets paved with gold upon their arrival, either. As Table 6 indicates, even during their third year in Canada immigrants live in generally less desirable housing conditions than long-term residents of the country. The fourth column shows a consistently smaller percentage of these newcomers owning their homes than is true for a representative Canadian control group that was matched on age, sex, occupation, and to some degree, region; hence the array of minus signs. Instead, they live more often either in boarding houses (if they arrive singly) or in apartments (if they arrive, like East and West Indians or Filipinos, in families).

Nonetheless there is hope, even in house-owning. The degree to which various immigrant groups approach the norm mainly reflects their economic circumstances upon entry.[12] British immigrants, who do best in this respect, were also best off when they arrived. Moreover, the very low scores of the Filipinos and West Indians do represent some house-owning only three years after arrival.

In addition, and perhaps most importantly for this book, the shortfalls cannot be attributed wholly to race. In terms of their frequency of house-owning, Japanese, East Indian, and Chinese newcomers to Canada all

Table 6
Departures from Normal Housing Accommodations
Among Third-Year Immigrants

	Boarding House	Apartment	Rented House	Own House
Italians	+32	−5	+5	−29
Ukrainians (USSR)	+17	+5	−1	−20
Chinese	+18	+1	+14	−29
Japanese	+16	+2	+11	−24
East Indians	+7	+25	−2	−25
Filipinos	+15	+33	+3	−45
West Indians	+4	+46	−4	−42
British	+1	+12	+7	−17
French	−3	+41	−2	−31

N.B. A plus (+) sign means that the immigrant group is higher than a representative Canadian control group on that particular type of accommodation by the number of percentage points specified. A minus (−) sign means that the immigrant group is lower to the same extent.

Source: Computed from data in *Three Years in Canada* (Ottawa: Information Canada, 1974), pp. 65-66.

do as well as, or better than, recent Italian and French immigrants. And they are within hailing distance of the British. These mundane economic data, based as they largely are on the entrants' resources and self-help, are a bright sign for the future.

NOTES

[1] As used in this chapter, "provinces" denotes "provinces and territories."

[2] Three groups, briefly considered in the text and not listed by name in census reports, are omitted. These are Métis, migratory workers, and European refugees. Reasons for using 1971 figures, and problems in updating them imaginatively are stipulated in Chapter 1.

[3] While not all West Indian immigrants are Black, apparently most are.

[4] We use 1971 provincial totals even though 1976 totals are now available, since the percentages that would be obtained from dividing 1971 ethnic figures by 1976 totals have no obvious meaning.

[5] Since we have rounded, this means that the particular minority contributes less than 1.5 percent to the province's population.

[6] See in particular Lyon, Peyton V., and Tareq Y. Ismael, eds., *Canada and the Third World* (Toronto: Macmillan of Canada, 1976).

[7] We do not consider the current efforts in Quebec to force Italian children into French language schools to be a special form of discrimination addressed against them.

[8] This is less true of recent arrivals from Africa and the West Indies. Before then, Black residents in Canada had pretty well lost their ancestral heritage and, for better or worse, were operating within the cultural confines of the encapsulating white society.

[9] Cf. Lipset, Seymour Martin, *Political Man: The Social Bases of Politics* (Garden City, N.Y.: Doubleday and Company Inc., 1960), Chapter 5.

[10] These ameliorative trends since World War II are discussed in our second volume.

[11] See also the discussion of this issue in Chapter 2.

[12] Other factors play a part too, for example, the stock of housing available for purchase and the culturally shaped priorities of the different groups.